WINNER ALRIGHT

Skinner Alright

GW00702121

Brendan Kelly

Acknowledgements

My thanks to all those who helped make this book become a reality. I particularly pay thanks to all those who became syndicate members with me over the years.

Thanks especially to my great friend Mark Kane from Dublin who not only typed every word of the script from my hand writing which in itself was a huge achievement but who also gave me the encouragement to put pen to paper in the first place following numerous conversations we had as former work colleagues over the years. To my younger brother Gerry of Colour Books who took on the project of designing and printing the book as a favour for me,without him I could not have progressed. To my family Vera, Erica and Jason for all the times I drove them mad asking for opinions on the different chapters and for the tea and biscuits brought to me as I wrote for hours on end. I also wish to thank my mother for being the very first person to read the early drafts and for her honest feedback such as taking out some four letter words here and there. To local writer John McKenna for taking time out from a very busy schedule and reading the complete draft prior to me sending it to Gerry. You may not be aware John but that Saturday you rang me to say that you thought it was a great read and very well written and that you actually read every word as a result was music to my ears at a time when things were getting me down. Finally to all the people mentioned in the book not least my Da god rest him for all of the stories and great memories of horseracing we shared together and for all of my friends who had great faith in me completing the project any time I discussed it with them.

Contents

Humble Beginnings

I was born into a family of thirteen children, ten brothers and two sisters, two sets of twins included. My poor sister Mary (twin of John) grew up with nothing but boys/men around her all of her early life until the last child born - would you believe was a little girl, my sister Siobhan who today is in her 30's and thank God we are all still here with the exception of my poor old Da, who sadly passed away aged 77 on 6th February 2005, a date I will never ever forget as we all loved the man to bits as did everyone he ever met.

My Da Harry (Har) was an out-and-out gentleman, a very dapper man who somehow or another in the midst of raising such a large family in 50's / 60's Ireland when life was hard and money scarce, he always managed to keep himself looking well and with impeccable dress sense.

He worked for almost 40 years in the same job in 'The Asbestos' factory in Athy, Co. Kildare, working three shifts, days, evenings and nights on alternative weeks. The Asbestos (now Tegral Building Products) has been in the town all of my life and gave employment and still does to a large number of local families. It was a very different place to work in my father's time and the very word 'Asbestos' says it all. In today's environment of 'Environmental Health & Safety' the conditions and lack of personal protective equipment in my Da's working career would have been completely unacceptable, thank God. However, even though when Da died he suffered from 'Asbestos' of the lungs, I know that both him and my mother were eternally grateful for such a steady and secure job allowing them to live a life and rear a family. Mind you, I simply don't know how they ever managed it. Ireland in those times was a different place and large families were common practice.

My mother for all her hardships and child-minding from the age of 17 always had one unique and tremendous asset as did my Dad actually and that was their youthful good looks. Even in the hardest of times none of us were aware that anything was ever wrong as my parents always looked well and we always had fun in the house regardless, a two-bedroom council cottage in Fortbarrington, Athy, Co. Kildare, approx. two miles from the town centre. A bathroom, kitchen etc. were built on over the years and Mam still lives there today with my brother Paddy who was the only one of us never to marry. The only one with sense I often say to my wife. Paddy moved back home after Da passed away so that Mam would not be alone. I have to say I admire Paddy so much for doing so and it's been good for him also as he spends lots of time tending to the large garden and has the place looking like the lawns of Buckingham Palace. He has also renewed acquaintances with old friends and will be found any Thursday, Friday, Saturday or Sunday in 'Purcell's' (the local pub) enjoying his pint of Guinness or maybe even a few of them, a trait he didn't lick from the ground nor did any of the rest of us. My Da loved his pint and thankfully right up to the end he was able to enjoy it. He died suddenly in his bed (which he always said would be his preferred way to go) and while it was hard on those left behind it did allow him to have a good life right to the end and not be stuck in a hospital with serious illness for his latter years. Instead his latter years were the best time of his life in a sense allowing him and Mam a bit of peace and quiet for a change. He was an avid Kildare GAA supporter and absolutely loved the horses, racehorses that is.

The horses! I picked up lots of traits from Da in every sense of the word and I'm often slagged by my wife Vera and my two kids Jason (19) and Erica (22) in lots of aspects of everyday life. Too long in the bathroom, clothes have to be perfect even if only going to the shop, the bit of hair (when I had it) never out of place. "Jesus you're the very same as your father!' sometimes the three of them together I hear. I am mad into most sports, have followed Kildare GAA all my life. I would dearly have loved to see Kildare win the All-Ireland final with my Da but unfortunately I never got to do so. 1998 we got to the final but Galway ruined a very special day for all of the Kelly clan. Some little things live with one forever and two of them in my life happened that day for me. The first was when we went for a pint before the match in O'Mahony's. When we were coming out the door of the pub heading for Croke Park (the home of GAA football), I held the door open for an old man who must have been at least 85 years old and as he passed by Jason (Jay) who was 9 at the time he asked Jay was it his first time to see Kildare in an All-Ireland final to which Jay replied 'Yes' and the old man said: 'It's mine as well'. I remember thinking to myself 'Jesus that sums up Kildare football over the years alright'. The second was at half-time in the match when we were well on top I went out for a cup of tea and on my way back to my seat with Jay the game had just re-started and Padraig Joyce of Galway scored a vital goal just before we sat down. Jay and I together said: 'Well, feck that anyway' and I have to say it made me laugh to a certain degree to hear my 9-year old sounding like me and I can guarantee you that my Dad who was in a different section of the stands with my eldest brother Eddie was muttering the same words 'Well, feck that anyway' with his son. Here's hoping that we'll have a *Sam Maguire Cup* paraded through the streets of Athy and all other towns in Kildare before I'm 85.

'The Horses'. Horseracing has been a huge part of my life ever since I was a child and not because we ever had horses or anything. It all stems from my Da loving a bet I think but then again I'm not sure as some of my brothers wouldn't bother watching a race if it was on in the back garden, never mind looking up breeding of certain winners etc.

But for me and some of my brothers I have always had a passion for horseracing. My Da often went to *The Curragh* which is the H.Q. of Irish Flat Racing. I remember as a young lad how I loved the place. Watching the horses in the parade ring, seeing all the famous jockeys such as Lester Piggott, Pat Eddery, Wally Swinburn, Christy Roche, to mention but a few. Da was a Pat Eddery fanatic and I remember asking him 'If Pat Eddery had a donkey in the race would you still back him?' after the horse had been beaten and I remember his answer being 'I think he had one in that race, son'.

Da had some brilliant sayings regarding horses. He would back a horse and say 'I hope that other one doesn't win and if he does I'll ate me you know what.' Many a time when the horses were nearing the finish I remember saying to him: 'You'd better take it out Da' and running away as I said it. Funny thing is I use the same saying today and have often had Erica and Jay telling me the same thing after a race.

Another of his sayings was after he'd backed a real slow horse he'd say: 'That yoke wouldn't run to scatter his own shit'. Mind you, I heard my Jay say that many times recently.

You see when Da worked in *The Asbestos* every week he got paid somehow or another he would always give Ma the few bob to keep the family show on the road and prevent a small-scale famine in the Athy area. But he always had the price of a few pints and a few bob to speculate on the horses. Indeed one of the very few times he gave me advice was 'Always make sure you've a few bob in your pocket, you'd never know when you might like a pint or back a winner'. Is it any wonder I've a simple attitude to life?

He would meet up with his work colleagues in Benny Carroll's pub for a pint and back a few horses most Thursdays and anytime he won a few bob you'd hear him whistling coming down the yard on his bike with a bag full of lollipops, crisps and chocolate for all of us and a few bob for Mam to buy something nice or pay some bill she was worrying about.

Every Thursday he met with the likes of Die Hard Dunne, Paddy Leonard, Jim Barr, Susie Owens and many more. Had a few pints, backed a few horses, shared a few stories and jokes and maybe the odd song or two, came home, had his bit of grub and had a joke and a bit of fun with all of us. Regardless of whether he won or lost or was drunk or sober, he was always in great form and many a night we sang 'The Wild Rover' or 'The Curragh of Kildare' together, especially the nights after he backed a few winners and after we'd stuffed ourselves from the plastic bag of goodies.

Looking back we had some great *craic* growing up in that house. I have no doubt in my mind that my love for horses is as a result of all the many happy times we had with Da. I'm sure all of the lads and Mary, Siobhan and of course Ma have different happy memories but the one that stuck with me is the memory of going racing, talking for hours about such a jockey, trainer or a particular horse and later on their progeny on the track.

My 2nd eldest brother called after my Da Harry also loves the horses as do my brothers John and Tony older than me and Davy the youngest boy. All the others including Ma will always back the odd time such as Cheltenham, the Grand National, the Derby etc. My son Jason who is currently in college studying commerce and Italian would give up college in the morning if we let him and go work with horses as he absolutely adores them. I've advised him to get his degree so that he always has something to fall back on whatever he decided to do. My daughter Erica has her law degree and is studying to be a solicitor. I suppose it was *my* way of advising them to 'always have a few bob in their pocket just in case they ever want a pint or ever need to back a horse!' I hope they both get their just rewards for all of their hard work and efforts.

As for me well I left school early so that I could bring in a few bob to the Mam to keep the wolf away from the door and give Da a bit of support for all his years of hard work and keeping the same wolf away as did most of my brothers and sisters. The younger members of the family were given the option of going on to college thanks to the extra few bob coming in from the older ones and some of them did go and thankfully did well as a result.

We all had nicknames growing up such as Ronnie, Corky, Prunch, Nay, Bonn, Fats and many more but mine was Skin/Skinner and still is today as is my son Jay's. When anybody says hello Brendan to me it takes me a split-second to realise it's me they're talking to, such is the manner in which the nickname Skinner stuck.

I got the name as results of a haircut from my father when I was about 11 or 12 I think. Back then all we did all day long was play football in Georgie Farrell's field, from the time we finished school to the time we went to bed. One day while we were playing, Da called us in one by one to cut our hairs on a chair in the middle of the kitchen floor as was often the case. No money back then to send us all for wash, cut and blow-dry. For some reason this day he went to town on my head as I had a head of wavy curls and he *skint* me (for value I reckon).

Around this time in Ireland most teenagers were into the skinhead era and as soon as I went back out to play ball my friend and neighbour Charlie Pender shouted out 'Fuck me pink - look at Skinner Kelly!' The rest is history.

I started working when I was 16 and followed in my brother Eddie's footsteps as a stores-person in the motor trade. Eddie was assistant manager in the Ford garage in Carlow at the time and was married and living in Carlow. I hitched for 3 years and was lucky to meet Paddy Conway who worked in Carlow and was from Athy so he gave me a lift for years. Thanks again Paddy. Eventually I was able to buy a Mk I Escort second-hand for myself for 850 pounds Hic 450 and Vera (my wife today) and I drove around for a few years in it. I remember getting a stereo fitted after a while and with Bruce Springsteen tapes blaring I thought I was deadly. Mind you, Bruce is still playing in my current car on CD I hasten to add 35 years later.

During those 35 years I've worked hard in various stores/inventory control jobs and have enjoyed trying to have a nice house, a nice-ish car, try give my wife and kids as much as I could and be a good father and husband like my Da before me.

In recent years I've been lucky enough to pay off the mortgage and have the kids in college, one finished and both nearly reared I suppose. So I started to think about Number One again you could say. Vera is constantly updating the nice house and she works hard herself and deserves all the home comforts she can get.

I got myself a nice car, nothing too extravagant or anything and at 47 after 16 years in my current job I've decided to opt for voluntary redundancy and start a new job.

Five years ago I decided to get involved in something that has always been a dream of mine and you may have guessed it involves horses. Probably the biggest mistake of my life but if I had not tried it now I never would and the rest of the book is all about my quest to own a winner in Ireland. There's an old saying 'If I knew then what I know now!' Well I suppose it's true but I'm still trying and that elusive one winner of my own is my dream and if it ever happens knowing my luck with horses to date I will probably die of heart failure as she crosses the finishing line but here's hoping she does and I won't. And if it never happens well at least I gave it a go and have the stories as a result.

I started writing this book during a holiday to a little place in Turkey called *Bitez*. If you ever get the chance I would advise you to pay it a visit as it is absolutely beautiful. Right now I am sitting by the beach with Vera in 40c plus, being attended to by a waiter named Ali who looks like an outbacker from Australia. Ali is a very friendly Turkish waiter who will not believe that I am writing a book about horses and has asked me for a signed copy to prove I really did write it. I look forward to giving him a copy as in this heat even writing is a strenuous task. Vera is fast asleep beside me which right now looks a far better and easier option.

Innocent Ireland. This picture was taken around the year 1964 and includes eight of us out playing with the cousins and neighbours on the road.
Back (L to R): Eddie, Willie Davitt, Harry, Mickey Dunne, Leo Dunne,
Philip Kenny, John (with our dog spot).
Front (L to R): Tony, Eamon Dunne, Francis (with Sandy),
myself (the baby of the family then), Paddy, Mick and Charlie Pender.

Off to Goffs Sales

When I decided to get involved in racehorse ownership I discussed it with Jay and my brother-in-law Marc and between us we came up with a plan to try a mare in foal at Goffs bloodstock sales in Kill, Co. Kildare. Marc had years of experience in this sphere of horse-racing and I was lucky that my father-in-law Eamon had a farm in Athy which he had transformed into a successful breeding operation for thoroughbred horses known as Fortbarrington Stud Farm. Eamon had always said that my Jay was a natural around horses and that someday I should try buy a nice mare and maybe breed a few foals from her, sell them on and maybe keep one at some stage for racing for ourselves. So the plan was for Jay, Marc and I to do just that.

So off we went to Goffs, Ireland's and indeed the world's premier thoroughbred sales arena. The sales consisted of hundreds of mares in foal so there was quite a lot of preparatory work in studying the sales catalogue in detail and marking the various mares we were interested in. We spent weeks doing so as there is so much to take into consideration. We wanted a young mare from which we could breed a few foals and if possible we wanted one who had actually won herself on the track. One with a strong pedigree was a must with some *black type* on her page. Black type meaning that some of her immediate family had actually won or been placed in top class races known in the game as group or listed type.

We also wanted one in foal to a top-class stallion and one who was carrying an early foal as in a foal due to be born around Feb, March, April latest the following year. All of these factors were a must in reducing the risk going forward and trying to breed quality stock from day one.

The problem was though that in order to tick all of these boxes we would need plenty of money as top quality mares don't come cheap. Needless to say we did not have lots of money so we were hoping for a bargain buy of a quality type. Our budget between us was £20,000 which to me was a lot to spend on any horse but in the rich man's game of horse breeding this was a small amount so we said a few prayers and hoped for the best.

The sales began on a Monday and as is customary we went to view the ones we had in mind on the Sunday. I felt excited about the prospect of picking up a really good one against all the odds and my Jay was like a young child heading to his/her first circus.

The first mare we viewed was one which I had marked myself and as soon as her handler walked her out of the stable, me being me I wanted her straight away. She was a large black mare heavy in foal to a group-one winning stallion. She had a shine on her coat and it was obvious to me that she had been very well cared for. When she came out of the stable to the paddock area she danced and skipped and the young man showing her was at his very best to hold her. I asked the lads what they thought of her as they were the experts and I was only the boy when it came to knowing horses. Marc thought she was nice but was a bit concerned about her temperament and thought she may be difficult to handle when foaling as a result. This would be her first foal and to be honest I didn't need any hassle once we had bought one so I was a bit reluctant to get involved. Jay thought she was grand (that's my Jay - full of info) but said we have lots more to view before any decisions would be made. We decided to mark her for consideration and moved on to our next port of call. We must have looked at another hundred mares later in the day and whatever about the two experts I was totally confused.

Monday morning 6:30am with a white frost covering the ground we cleared the ice from the car window and off we headed back to Goffs and today was D-Day. We had all of our homework done - now all we needed was the stroke of luck which would be the difference between success and failure. The excitement was fever pitch and the butterflies were eating the belly out of me in anticipation of what was to come. For the 40-minute journey from home we spoke of nothing else but horses. Mind you the three of us are fairly good at that.

When we got to Goffs the sales had everything ready to kick off at 10am and we still had a few more to look at before then. No time for any delaying at this stage. I suggested breakfast and nearly got the head taken off me. 'I can't function without breakfast', so off I went alone and rushed a couple of slices of toast with two rashers and a nice mug of tea followed by a smoke and caught up with the experts to continue the viewing exercise.

I remember asking Marc and Jay had they a preference at this point and they both said 'not really' to my surprise. I thought myself 'how the hell do I know which ones to bid for?' as it was now 9:30am and just a half-an-hour before show-time.

The black mare I had shown preference to entered the sales ring quite early in the day and we watched her sell for £19,000 and I couldn't help but think we should have bought her. Just a gut feeling on my behalf but more to follow on this later .

The first one the boys asked me to bid on was a class act who was bred in the purple and in foal to the king of all stallions *Sadler's Wells*.

'Don't let her go without having at least a look' says Jay, 'you'd never know nobody might want her'.

'Yeah right' says I but I proceeded to do what I was told. Before the auctioneer got the first sentence from his lips there was a bid of £100,000 put on her by some aul fella wearing a turpin. 'It's gonna be a long day'says I.

Lots more followed and while most were out of our league there were a few however who did sell for reasonable money so I wasn't giving up quite yet. The problem however in such situations is making up your mind as regardless of which one you decide on you're always gonna be afraid it's the wrong horse. Horses are a gamble as far as I'm concerned so no matter which way we turned we were gambling our luck.

I'll tell you something for nothing. One would want to be in the full of their health at the sales especially when considering buying. It was now almost 5pm and the sales was on for three days. I thought I'd be home rubbing down our new horse at this stage. Instead we hadn't even put in a bid. We did manage to get a bit of lunch though which I was pleasantly surprised about.

Six o'clock passed, as did 7pm and to be frank I was totally pissed off and knackered. 7.20pm on the clock and Jay runs over to me and says excitedly: 'Right Da are ya right?' I thought we were going home but no. We walked hurriedly to the pre-sales ring and there she was. 'That's her, Da!' says Jay. 'Yeah' says Marc 'that's her, Skinner!'

An outstanding-looking bay mare with a white stripe on her face Lot No called *Curtsey.* She had a nice pedigree, was by *Mark of Esteem,* a group-one winning sire and was carrying a foal by *Soviet Star* himself a group winner and from one of the strongest families in thoroughbred racing.

'We'll never get her, lads, she's a cracker' says I, 'she'll make a fortune'.

'Don't start' says a cranky Jay at this hour of the evening – 'All we can do is try!'

When she eventually entered the ring the bidding was brisk but there was hope as it did slow down a bit at around £18k. Marc asked me in the middle of bidding 'What's the most we'll go, Skin?' I made a quick call to the boss at home and she says if you think she's worth it go to £25k. All of these discussions took place in a matter of seconds as the horse was being sold at the same time. I was a bundle of nerves and Marc took over the bidding on our behalf as I was rubbing my hand so much the lads were afraid that the auctioneer might see it as a bid and I'd end up bidding against myself. We were conscious that the vendor may have been bidding up the price to make it better for him but we had made up our minds that £25k was our limit. When we got to £25k it was our bid and somebody went '25 and a half'. 'Feck ya' says I and I looked at Marc £26k and that was it no more. The auctioneer took a fuckin' eternity to try attract more bids but eventually got to the point of 'going once, going twice' wait for a minute or so and 'thank you sir, I hope she gives you a derby winner'. Curtsey was ours. I needed a smoke, I needed a pint, I needed a bloody ambulance', truth be told. Jay, Marc and I shook hands, group-hugged and the journey had begun. We went out and met Curtsey, got her loaded in the horse-box and thanks be to God we were off home with our prize asset. It was dark when we got home and we put her into the stable for the night and went home ourselves as we were too exhausted to go for a pint. Hard work this buying horses and I was due back at my job at 7:00am next morning. Marc and Jay were up at the crack of dawn and put her out in the paddocks with Eamon's other mares and eventually she settled down nicely. Jay was out before and after school for months putting her in and out in the winter months. The hard part of the breeding operation that is. Regardless of how good or bad horses are they still have to be fed and watered and their beds cleaned out each morning.

Curtsey was a really lovely-looking mare. She took to Jay as all horses do. Any time I went near her she nearly ' killed me but once Jay was happy I was. Story of my life 'Once Jay and Erica are happy I'm fine'. We didn't have a real bad winter and Curtsey thrived and was very well minded by all and sundry. The months flew by and before we knew it Curtsey was due her first foal and I remember waiting was the very same as when I waited for the birth of our two children.

Eamon had a special foaling box with video camera which could be monitored from the house. It was equipped with infra-red heating lights suspended from the rafters. A very close eye was kept on Curtsey during the day waiting for her to show signs of foaling, such as *waxing up* which is the term used for the build-up of milk in the mare. She was due to foal mid-April and for weeks we waited, until the very last day of the month. There was great excitement tinged with nervousness that all would go ok. Jay's eyes never left that monitor for one minute and he waited for hours for nights into the early hours of the morning. I was at home in my bed waiting for the call and eventually on a cold April morning at approx. 2:30am Jay rang to say 'Hurry up, Da, she's started!' I'm only 10 minutes drive from the stud so I was there in 5.

It took forever to happen and I have to say it is nature at its' very best to see a full-size foal with its' long legs, big neck and large head come from the relatively small-sized belly in comparison but there she was. We had hoped for a colt (male) as they are more valuable but we didn't mind the filly once everything was ok. It's a tricky time when it's the mare's first foal as she is not too sure what's going on at first. It is vital that she bonds straight away with the foal and that the foal starts to drink from the mum as soon as possible. Once this happens nature takes over.

Curtsey however was not the best mum in the world and even though she cleaned off the foal etc. there was no way she was having her drink from her and just kicked her out of the way each time the foal tried to. Thank God Eamon was there as I was panicking a little and thinking that the foal was now a couple of hours old and needed to drink soon. I had flashbacks of Marc telling me that the black mare may be problematic at this stage but here we were with the problem from the chosen mare. We put the rope on Curtsey's head collar and Marc held her. I was given the job of holding up her front leg to prevent her kicking the foal away with her hind ones. No easy job at 5am in the morning, holding up a fully-grown horse's leg!!! Eamon and Jay guided the foal towards the mare's udder and I swear to God with the sweat trickling into my eyes I prayed that the fussy bitch would let her daughter drink. The weight of her leg after a while was pulling the arms out of me. The lads tried and tried and tried and tried and tried again and fair play to them eventually it worked and the sound of that foal sucking will live forever in my mind. I was never as happy to take my hand off a leg in all my life. I could see the tears swell in Jay's eyes and even Marc and Eamon who saw all this type of thing before were thrilled that mother and daughter were doing fine at last. Well, that was it and within a couple of hours our little *Soviet Star* was walking around as though she was a month old. She was a gorgeous bay foal with a very appropriate star-shaped white mark on her head. She was a very well-made and compact foal and we knew there and then that she would grow to be a smashing individual who just might pay us back on our initial investment on her mother. Well that was the plan anyway. For months my Jay would only be found in one place, and you can all guess where that was. He was absolutely stone-mad about her and she adored him also. Marc and I, two grown men were also quite smitten with her and before I knew it Curtsey had to be brought only a couple of weeks later to a new stallion to be covered for her second foal. Full-time job or what?!! And by the way these stallions don't come cheap. That was another day's work plus we had to decide on one in such a short space of time. No pressure eh?!!

The three of us decided to go for a first season sire in the hope that the one we picked would turn out to be a revelation throwing winners of top-quality races in his first crop of foals. This in turn would automatically add to the value of our foal when he or she came along the following spring. There were lots to choose from and all of the ones we considered were famous racehorses from the track just starting out on their stud careers. Jay in particular combed the stallion books, internet and any other form of statistical information available. If he puts as much effort into his college exams he will turn out to be a genius.

Eventually after lots of discussion we narrowed the list down to three. Each of us had our own preferences and we decided to visit the three stud farms where the final three stood. Gilltown Stud, just outside the town of Kilcullen, Co. Kildare was our first point of call to see the multiple group one and Breeder's Cup winner *Kalanisi*. In his first season he stood at a cost of €15,000 (good money if you can get it and a lot for us to come up with at the time having bought Curtsey) but if we wanted to stick to the plan and try breed quality then this was a small fee as such for such a prolific horse.

The stud groom asked us to wait outside the stabling barn as he went to bring Kalanisi out for us to view. I don't know about the lads but I was gobsmacked by the sheer beauty of the place with its' pristine lawns and fabulous views across the large grazing paddocks with its' mature oak trees providing both beauty and shelter for the horses outside. To be honest I don't think the two lads even noticed as they were watching for the groom to come back like two kids waiting for their mam to come back from the shop with ice-cream.

After a few minutes we could hear the sound of horseshoes clipping over the cobbled area of the barn and then he appeared.

Kalanisi. Jesus what a specimen of a horse! Standing in front of us amidst the beauty of Gilltown stud I said to Marc and Jay: 'We won't get much nicer than him, lads'. The groom, a nice young fella asked us:

'What do ya think, lads?'

'Nice horse', says Jay, 'can you walk him up a bit for us please?'

My Jay looked like Robert Sangster at Keeneland Sales as he

watched every move Kalanisi made as he walked then trotted along in a kind of show-off way as much as to say '*look at me aren't I brilliant?* sort of way. We thanked the groom for his time and before we left we visited the stables of other famous stallions standing there at that time. We got to see *Daylami* and *Sinndar*, two very famous horses also. For anybody as interested in racing as we were, this was a cracker of a day out. We headed back to the car and discussed Kalanisi in detail and decided to hold our decision until after we saw our others on the shortlist. It was a Saturday afternoon and I'd had a busy week in work and had a few jobs to do at home so I told the lads that we'd head home and maybe see the others during the week.

That night Marc called to our house and himself and Jay had a chat in the kitchen and afterwards they said to me:

'What do you think of giving Kalanisi a go, Skin?'

I said he has to be worth a try' so that was it.

A few days later Curtsey was on her way to Gilltown to meet her new boyfriend. It normally only takes a day or so for the covering to take place but Curtsey was a very awkward individual when it came to it. She came in and out of season quite quickly and as a result had to spend a week at Gilltown in order to catch her at the right time. Thankfully it all worked out in the end and we had her scanned soon afterwards and there on the vet's monitor was our next baby-in-waiting. We were delighted. I wasn't too happy when I got the bill from Gilltown though which included a week to ten days B&B for Curtsey which added over a grand to the €15k. We didn't have to pay straight away so by the time we did pay I managed somehow or another to come up with the money. Vera told us we were mad and hoped it all worked out for us. I said three Hail Mary's every night that it would.

So now we had our Soviet Star foal and we had Curtsey carrying the Kalanisi foal. Things were happening rather quickly as we went from having no horses to having two-and-a-bit. They spent most of the time in the paddocks, weather permitting so all we had to do now was keep a close eye on them and as the Soviet Star grew her feet were constantly manicured by the blacksmith. This is crucial in the early growth of racehorses as it keeps their legs straight etc. which in turn give them the proper conformity required to race. Now I'm no expert when it comes horses but that's what the lads told me.

Matagorda

A round this time Eamon had a few yearlings which he had kept back for racing or to sell at the yearling sales. One night we got chatting and he asked me if I would be interested in a free lease with one of them to maybe set up a racing syndicate with a few friends from work. I work in Newbridge in Kildare, which is only a mile from The Curragh racecourse, which is one of the racing world's premier racecourses. A lot of the lads I work with are from the area and fanatics when it comes to horses. I asked around for a few weeks if any of them would be interested in becoming involved in a racing syndicate taking a free lease on a nice filly. The response was immediate and within a short space of time I had seven definite names including my sister Siobhan and her husband Steven plus a few of the lads from work. My brother Dave, Jay and I made it ten members and to make a long story short 'Ten Racing Syndicate' became a reality. A free lease means that Eamon still owned the horse but she would run under the banner of 'Ten Racing' and we would share the training fees and any prize money during her racing career. If she ever won any that is. It is an interesting concept in racing today and indeed syndicates of all types have been the life-blood of Irish racing. They allow the ordinary working man to become involved in ownership of a share in a racehorse so quite a few people in Ireland now own a leg or a tail or a head of a horse.

The syndicate look after every aspect of the horse's racing career. They register the horse with *Horse Racing Ireland* (HRI) who are the governing body of Irish racing. The syndicate name the horse, choose the racing colours, choose the trainer etc. They look after all of the admin cost involved from day one and they are also responsible for all training costs plus veterinary and blacksmith. It is important to be aware of all these costs before becoming involved as racing is a very, very expensive hobby, take it from me. Each syndicate must have one of its' members as the agent who looks after almost everything and who is the person who both HRI and the trainer liaise with. I decided to nominate one of the members as secretary who would manage all financial transactions on behalf of the ten members. It was only fair that I took up the task of agent as it was all my idea for better or worse and my good friend Paul (Hector) Foran became secretary and may I say at this point that he did an excellent job of it. Thanks Hec. So with everything in place officially we all had a look at the horse in question and all agreed she was a very nice filly with excellent breeding and closely related to a few previous winners, one who had been placed in group-company.

We spent a while deciding on what to call her and eventually I suggested *Matagorda* after a resort in Lanzarote which some of us had visited before. All the members thought it was a nice name so the yearling filly would run as Matagorda showing the race-card owner as 'Ten Racing Syndicate'. We decided on a Curragh-based trainer so in the space of a few weeks Matagorda commenced training with Michael (Mick) Halford who is one of the best in the business. It would be a few months before she would reach the track if ever as some of them never do. Mick had his work cut out with Matagorda as she turned out to be stubborn enough and there were days to quote Mick when he said: 'If I kissed her arse I still couldn't get her out the gate for her morning work some days'. However himself and the team persisted and about six months later Matagorda was entered for a couple of races in the calendar. There is a serious problem in Ireland today in that there are far too many racehorses and not enough race meetings so an entry does not automatically mean that your horse will get into the race. More about this at a later stage as it can be extremely frustrating.

Matagorda finally got into a two-year old maiden in Gowran Park racecourse which was close enough to home for us all so we were all hugely excited to see her name, our syndicate name and colours on the *Racing Post* newspaper that morning. All part and parcel of having a racehorse in your own name. My quest to own a winner had begun. The butterflies were back again. I forgot to mention by the way that at this point Matagorda had cost us about €10k just to get this far. Her first race was worth €15k in prize money and of course all the other members thought she would win first time out. Naturally enough I hoped they were right but from talking to Mick I knew he was just hoping for a good show from her today. No matter how often I told the others this they were still convinced she'd win. One of the biggest problems with syndicates – the expectation levels. However I'd seen miracle results in racing before and tried to be positive as well as realistic. Matagorda ran in the 1st race and would be ridden by a top Irish jockey in Seamus (Seamie) Heffernan so it was now in Seamie's hands and in the lap of the gods that she do well.

On the way to Gowran I was stopped for speeding by the Gardai even though Hector who had gone down before me had rang me to say that they were stopping for speeding and even gave me the exact location. I think the butterflies were working overtime at this point that I only had one thing on my mind and that was the race. The garda asked me why I was in a hurry and doing 75 in a 60mph area? I told him I had a runner in the 1st in Gowran and he asked: 'Does it have a chance?' Seeing my opportunity to avoid a speeding fine I said I hope she wins and proceeded to give him the horse's name etc. Fair play to him he said: 'well less of the speeding, you've loads of time', thanked me for the tip and sent me on my way. He was a nice fella actually.

Most of the syndicate members were able to attend this day and standing in the parade ring as owners was kinda special and I could see they were proud to be involved and there we were a bunch of ordinary 5/8s rubbing shoulders with the rich and famous. Well that's how it felt for us anyway. My brother Dave brought Da with him that day and little did I know that this would be the last race meeting I would ever have my Da God rest him with me. One of us took a photo of him in the stands studying form in the newspaper and the same photo takes pride of place on the mantelpiece at home in Fortbarrington today.

Well needless to say my nerves were shattered at this point as I felt responsible for having persuaded the others to become involved and I was hoping probably even more for them that Matagorda would do us proud. The horses left the parade ring and we watched our red & white colours go to post on the big screen. She went into the starting stalls without any fuss which I was quite pleased about and within seconds Des Scahill, course commentator called '*And they're off*'. The adrenalin had me pumping and I smoked a cigarette in two pulls. '*Such-a-one is in front followed by another followed by a few more and Matagorda brings up the rear*'. Don't panic yet, says I to myself and as they come around the bend at halfway '*such-a-one's in front followed by another followed by another followed by a few more and Matagorda still brings up the bloody rear*'. (He didn't say bloody I did). Two furlongs to go and she's still plum last and making no impression whatsoever. 'Well, ' says I something must be wrong. Jay put his head in his hands and said: Da what'll you say to the boys?'

'Thanks for that, Jay' says I as I walked away in disgust. However I gave her the benefit until I spoke to Seamie to see what he thought was amiss. We went back to the parade ring to meet him and I asked:

'Well, Seamie, what did you make of that?' hoping for some genuine explanation for such a poor run. Seamie's words which I'll always remember were:

'I think she might just be a bit too slow to be honest'.

Don't be afraid to tell me straight, Seamie, I thought to myself. Matagorda ran once more in Roscommon a few weeks later and finished 7th of 15 runners which I was happy enough with but Mick said the next day that she was very stiff in the back which he felt might always be the case when she raced so between the two of us on that call there and then we decided to pull her out of training. Matagorda has since had a few really nice-type foals by National Hunt (jump racing) stallions and they will begin racing when they reach 4 years old. It wouldn't surprise me if she bred a champion hurdle winner. I was disappointed for the syndicate members but they were great and all said: we all know it was a gamble from the start so don't let it bother you'. Matagorda unfortunately was not to be my first winner.

While the Matagorda era was taking place don't forget that we still had the Soviet Star growing in the paddocks and it was only weeks away until the foal sales in Goffs at this point for which we had her entered.

Off to Goffs (Again)

Preparation for Goffs this time was completely different as we were now the vendor as distinct from the buyer. The Soviet Star had turned into a peach of a foal and we felt well within our rights to put her in to the sales with a reserve tag of €20,000. Quite expensive for a foal from an unproven mare but we thought because she was so well-made that we might just get it. To be honest I needed a few bob back in between Matagorda, Curtsey, Kalanisi as I had spent a fortune just to get this far. Vera told me if any more money went into 'them horses' that she'd divorce me. I think she was telling the truth and deep down I know she was right which scared me a little.

We brought the Soviet Star to the sales on the Saturday for viewing on the Sunday along with a few more foals from Eamon's stud. Jay never left her side and I'd say he'd have spent the night in the stable with her had it been suggested. Back again on the Sunday to show her and she would be entering the sales ring on the Tuesday.

The number of people who came to view that foal between Sunday and Monday was incredible to say the least. Jay was worn out leading her by the time Tuesday came around. It was very encouraging to have so much interest and we were pleased about it. The sales started on Monday however and truth be told we were a bit disappointed with some of the prices even for foals who were better than ours. By late Monday evening it was obvious to us that it was a bit of a shite sales so we didn't expect to reach our reserve far from it to be honest. That night we decided that worse-case scenario if we didn't sell that the Soviet Star would become our next Matagorda. We would sell a few shares to get a few bob back in and give her the chance to become my first winner. She certainly looked good enough to be. Sorted, plan in place.

Tuesday morning 6am showered, shaved and on the road to Goffs. More lookers as soon as we got there. They'll all look I said to Jay but I bet you they want her for nothing. Jay must have walked two hundred miles that week-end and finally got to the sales ring late on Tuesday evening where the bidding begins. The Soviet Star, God help her must have been wrecked from all the walking but Jay kept her well watered and fed.

Mind you the bidding took off fairly lively in lots of €1,000 and before we knew it there was €10,000 on the board. It did slow down then but got to €14,500 before it stopped. Round and round the ring the auctioneer looked for more bids but stopped the hammer with a sigh of 'Sorry, not today Gentlemen'. *Bollox* I thought maybe we should've let her go. Some aul' fella followed us back to the stable and offered us €16,500 and again we said no. Driving home I thought bollox again and money in the bank and all that shite but I was disappointed. Eamon put my mind to rest when he said 'Don't worry, Skin, she'll cost you nothing in the field between now and next year, so you can decide between now and then what ye want to do with her'.

The Plan 'B' as previously discussed was the most likely option and he was right she was gonna be in the field till then, thanks to him at no expense.

For the next couple of months I gave the equine side of my brain a complete break. I switched off completely and concentrated on everyday life. I paid regular visits to the stud farm just to see how much the Soviet Star had grown and how Curtsey was coming along. I was enjoying just having them both and Jay was there nearly all the time helping out with all of the horses and the work associated with them. At the end of those couple of months it was decided that we would send the Soviet Star to Peter Reilly whose business was breaking in young flat horses and getting them ready for training in time for them to be ready to run as 2 year-olds.

The couple of months flew by and before we knew it our baby, who had long since been weaned from her mother, was off to learn all about her purpose in life. Racing. It would take Peter another few months to get her to the stage whereby she would be ready to enter a trainer's yard. It was exciting I have to say, particularly when she was our own foal. Peter was well-impressed with her and had good feeling about her as soon as he laid eyes on her. My only underlying fear during all this time is that it was all costing me a hell of a lot of money with no return. I had to think positive and keep focussed on why I was doing all this. I was following my dream and that of my son Jay's and having just the one son having watched my Da rear eleven of them I thought , all I can do is my best. I had supported Erica *(my Nick* I call her) all the way through college and still am with all of her required studies in the tough business of trying to become a solicitor so it wasn't as though I was showing favouritism towards Jay or anything of the sort. My Nick thought I was stone mad anyway trying to make the breakthrough into Irish Racing, as did Vera. Come to think of it, all of my family were of the same opinion: *You are mad Skinner.* I remember one of my first cousins Eamon Dunne telling me that horse racing in Ireland is a seriously rich man's sport for such as the Coolmore's, Sheikh Mohammed, Moyglare to mention but a few, all of whom were backed up by millions. How will an ordinary *gobshite* like you ever compete with the likes of them? No disrespect intended, he says. To sum it up, Skin, if those horses of yours were any good you wouldn't have them. I had to think about that one for a while but yes I could see his point. I thought to myself: Am I at nothing here, am I letting my heart rule my head and empty my wallet?? Why could I not take up bird-watching or something where all I'd need was a miserable pair of binoculars and I even had those already, for racing of course.

By now anyway I was hooked and I said no way am I not seeing this through now having come so far with the whole thing.

Within a matter of weeks the Soviet Star was broken in and being ridden everyday and she was becoming a proper little racehorse. Every time I went to see here I thought This is why I'm doing all this and the driving force behind it all was both Jay and my overwhelming desire and quest to own a winner. I wasn't looking to own a Derby or *Prix de L'arc* winner or anything, an upside-down handicap in Sligo would have done me so I would be doing my best to avoid some of the big guns along the way.

Things were going like clockwork with the Soviet Star and Marc was very upbeat about the whole thing which gave me some confidence. Peter was more than pleased with her progress and was of the opinion that she would be a nice *early-type* meaning she'd be ready to run at the very start of the flat season in mid-March. This was a huge bonus for us so we were all delighted with how the plan was going. I remember ringing Peter on a Wednesday morning on his mobile and he was actually sitting on the Soviet Star's back, having worked her when he answered. Both of us thought what a coincidental time for me to ring. He told me I couldn't have rang at a better time as he was chuffed with what she'd just done and said: 'I think you could have nice little filly here, Skin'. I felt like a young child after he'd said it. We said goodbye and I remember clenching my fist and saying aloud: 'Go on ya little daisy' after I'd put down the phone.

The following Saturday I was in work and at around 8:30am I went to the canteen for breakfast. I was in good form and had a large breakfast on my tray just approaching the till to pay for same when my mobile rang in my pocket. I saw it was Marc on the caller Id and straight away I sensed there was something wrong as Marc does not ring me that early especially at week-ends. Reluctantly I pressed the green answer button and said:

'Well, Marc, is everything alright?'

'Howya Skinner' he said *'I'm afraid it's not'* and immediately one hundred things raced through my mind as to what could be wrong.

'What is it, Marc?' I asked.

I knew by him that he had a lump in his throat as he spoke.

Next thing he said: *'Skin, the Soviet Star is dead'.*

Right there and then you could have knocked me down with a feather. The blood in my body went straight to my feet and I was speechless. Marc allowed me a minute or so to respond. I asked: 'What the hell happened?'

He said Peter had rang him to say that during the previous night she had become cast in her stable and in an effort to get to her feet she had panicked and broke her pelvis as she struggled to get up. This is a regular occurrence with horses and basically just means that they lie down in a silly position not allowing themselves enough space to get back on their feet. Panic naturally enough sets in and sometimes they are just unlucky to inflict irreparable damage upon themselves before anyone can help which in her case is exactly what happened. Unfortunately she had to be put down straight away to take here out of pain.

The young lady at the till could see by me that I'd had bad news and asked me if I was ok. I told here I was ok but didn't feel much like breakfast. She said leave the tray there and go and look after yourself. I think she may have suspected that there had been a death in the family. She was right.

After I'd said goodbye to Marc I needed a cigarette and I headed back to my locker, changed my shoes and decided to go home. I needed to get my head together. As soon as I got to the factory gate I lit up my cigarette and stopped outside while I smoked it and tried to think straight. Suddenly it hit me like a ton of bricks: *How am I going to tell Jay?* At that very moment I cried like a baby. I had to ring Vera and I knew by her that she was shocked and she asked how will we tell Jay and that he'd be devastated. I asked her to wait until I got home to say anything as Jay was in bed. I was home in 40 minutes and when I walked in Jay was crying at the kitchen table as Vera had to tell him when he got up. I put my arms around him and explained or at least tried to that there are worse things that can happen in life and though it may seem like the end of the world right now I tried to assure him that everything would be ok in the end. My fatherly words were as much for myself as they were for Jay. I told him we still had the Kalanisi to look forward to and he said: 'Ah I know, Da, I was just looking forward *so much* to her racing this season' and I said I know, so was I. It was a long day to say the least and lots of tears were shed before bed-time came around. I remembered late in the afternoon to ring the lads in work to explain my absence. They were wondering where I had disappeared to and were afraid of what was wrong as the lady from the till had asked them how I was earlier in the day. One of the lads, Kieran, said to me that it was hard luck but it could be a lot worse (my words to Jay) and I did take comfort from someone else saying it.

The next day I rang Peter and he was keen to point out that it was an accident and I told him I understood and was not blaming him in any way. He said he was very upset over the whole episode and for me not to worry about and bills owed and how to dispose of the horse, that he had looked after all of that.

I rang my Mam and she cried on the phone as she asked how was Jay. I spoke to my Da and he said you may just be positive that it was at times like this that you show how strong you are. Funny enough he was spot on as usual. My friend Hec rang me to say he had heard and how sorry he was and he mentioned some of the lads from Ten Racing were anxious to become involved when the Soviet Star had been ready for training if the opportunity was there. I thanked him for his support as a true friend and after we said goodbye I asked Jay if he was going to the local football match and I was delighted when he said: 'Yeah, we'll go'. It was the start of getting back to normal. On the way to the pitch in the car he said out of the blue: 'Are ya alright Da?' and I swear to God I loved him for it. I told him I was grand and jokingly I said:

'It'll make it all the sweeter when we do have our first winner, son'. He replied: 'Jaysus you're a gas man, Da'. It was all downhill from there and unfortunately the Soviet Star would not be my first winner and my quest would have to go on. Athy won the match however so at least something good happened that week-end. That same night I twisted and turned in my sleep thinking I should have taken the €16,500 or that I should have had her insured at least but fuck it, hindsight is a great thing and tomorrow was the first day in the rest of my life so onwards and upwards.

A few weeks passed and one day I received a sales catalogue from Tattersalls Ireland for their upcoming yearling sales. At first I thought 'You can feck off with your ' yearling sales' but I found myself flicking through the catalogue a few nights later just out of interest of course. *Yeah right, says you!!* For the next few days I thought about what Hec had said to me about the syndicate and got talking to a few of the members and the overall feeling amongst most of them was to buy our own horse this time and try again. They were so keen it was unbelievable. I told them about the upcoming sales in Tattersalls in November and they asked would I have a look and if there was a suitable filly would I be prepared to go again? I told them I'd have to think about it and would let them know. I was half-afraid to even mention it at home for fear of Vera shooting or stabbing me on the spot. I did eventually however and she said: 'Oh here we go again!' That was good enough for me. Jay of course was up for it and said he'd have a look at what fillies were available first. We thought it best to stick with fillies as in the event of them being useless which was the most likely scenario it may be easier to get rid of her for breeding purposes.

Penny and Me

I had met Mick Halford at the races somewhere and I told him about the Soviet Star etc. and that I was thinking of picking up a nice filly in Tattersalls to give it another try. I could see by him that he admired my optimism and as a gesture, a very nice gesture I hasten to add from such a high-profile and busy trainer he said: 'If you like, pick out a few that interest you and I'll have a look at them for you prior to the sales and who knows, I might see one myself for you'. I was thrilled skinny with Mick's offer and told him I might take you up on that and thanks a million.

As in everything with horseracing the time flew and all of a sudden Jay, Vera and I were off to the sales in Fairyhouse complex which is where Tattersalls hold all of their events. I had arranged to meet Mick in the afternoon as most of the lots I was interested in would not reach the ring till later that evening.

We looked at about twenty different ones. I think somewhere in the back of our minds we were using the Soviet Star as a benchmark, so none of them really came up to scratch in our opinion. I met Mick later on and told him I hadn't seen any in particular that we liked and he had a look at a few of them and agreed. He said he would have a scout around and see if he could recommend anything. He had my number and would give me a call if he found any. I heard nothing from him for most of the evening but around 6pm he asked me to meet him in the pre-parade ring. He showed us a filly by *Orpen* who is a very decent stallion and he explained to me that she had a full brother in training as a two-year old last year and that he had done o.k.-ish. At least it was a bit of a marker to go by. The amazing thing about the filly he was showing us was that the middle-aged gentleman leading her around was leading her from the wrong side and it looked very strange to me. I had never seen a horse being led from the right-hand side of the horse and both Jay and I didn't know what to make of it. Jokingly I said to Jay: 'Maybe he's a foreigner who drives on the opposite side'. Fair play to him anyway he kept her going no bother.

There wasn't much time to make up our minds but Mick thought she might be worth a try although he did say you have to be realistic and understand that she could be useless also. I thanked him for his advice and said I'd have a look and if she was within our budget we'd give it a lash.

The filly entered the ring and I was nervous enough about how it would go and don't you know mine was the last bid. Could this be the one?? I had made arrangements with a lady from Suncroft, Co.Kildare - Valerie, who was a pre-trainer, for her to collect a filly if I did purchase and with it being our first time to buy in Tattersalls I had to arrange a bank draft which meant the filly would stay overnight and be collected by Valerie and brought to her place for pre-training straight away. Vera would organise the bank draft and gave it to Valerie the next morning. Before we left the sales Mick advised me to have a vet test the filly's wind which I did and it was here I got to meet the man who led her around. He was indeed a foreigner by the name of Hans (I was right) who kept saying to me in a type of Norwegian accent: 'You got her for nothing'. I said there's no such thing in racing and he laughed. He was a lovely man and I had to ask him why he led her from the right to which he replied: 'I don't know whether it was her or me but neither of us could move forward from the left'. I had visions of Rory Cleary or Johnny Murtagh riding side-saddle to get this filly to run.

Valerie picked her up the next day and the team called to see her later in the week and gave the seal of approval and each paid their share within days to cover the bank draft. Jay and I held the major share and would pay the costs based on percentage owned. In conversation I said: 'Right lads we're going forward again' and there and then Hec said that's the new name for the syndicate - *Going Forward Racing* and that was that. Jay said I hope we don't end up calling it *Going Backwards!* My luck to date the latter may have been the one to use. Anyway we were off again and in the coming months we would register both new syndicate and new horse.

How hard can it be to name a bloody horse?? I'll tell you this much, with seven different people involved it can be unbelievably difficult. There were all sorts put forward and two or three members would say 'Yes, that's a good one' and the others would say 'that's a brutal name'. Britney Spears was in the news at the time and I suggested *Mrs. Federline* as the name but same story a few agreed and the remainder said *brutal.* In the end I suggested each member give in one name and we would vote on them as a group. Do you think they could even do that? Jesus they were doing my head in and those who rejected the names put forward were the very ones who had no suggestions at all.

This went on for weeks. One of the lads rang me and suggested *Snowy*. I said: 'Snowy what?' 'Just Snowy', he said. 'Will ya feck off with yer Snowy' says I, 'this is a *racehorse* not a bloody labrador pup!' He said: 'Right, don't ate me I was only trying to be helpful'. We had a good laugh about it. *Snowy* eh??!! It was almost time to register the name and I wouldn't mind but to do so I needed three which is compulsory on the application form, should those suggested be already in use. *Snowy* might come in handy yet.

Jay was watching *MTV* on telly a few nights later and a song came on from a young American band called *Hanson* and the name of the song was 'Penny and Me'. Jay shouted in to me in the kitchen.

'*Da, I think I have a name for the horse*'.

I said: 'What is it this time? It better be a better one than Snowy'.

He shouted in '*Penny and Me*' and I asked him:

'Where the hell did that come out of?'

'*It's the name of the song there on the telly*'.

It was a very catchy song and I thought a very catchy name. Straight away I made seven phone calls and hey presto – 'Penny and Me' would be the one to continue our quest for a winner. 'Fair play to ya, Jay' says I and filled out the form there and then. I used two titles of Bruce Springsteen songs for choices two and three and didn't bother with Snowy, just in case. *Snowy!!* The name was later accepted and we were back in business.

I left Penny with Valerie to have her broken and prepared for the track and Mick would take her in when it was time. I rang Mick and everyone was happy with these arrangements. Valerie starting working on Penny after about a month or so and Penny turned into a huge filly, completely different from anything I'd had in training before. Mick was delighted with her progress when he called to see how she was coming along. He was of the opinion that she wouldn't run till mid-summer or so and agreed to take her in for full training around end of February/early March which suited us fine.

Penny's full brother who was now a 3 year-old was back in training also, so it was interesting to see how he would get on. It was Jay's job to keep an eye on the entries once the season began which was March so it was only a couple of months away which would fly by. Indeed they did. I decided with the benefit of experience at this stage that I would keep my expectations low this time and be prepared for whatever was thrown at me in the coming months in the volatile world of thoroughbred horse-racing. I took a step back and left everything to Valerie and Mick and hoped for the best. I did my best to persuade all of the other members to do likewise which in fairness they did.

It was now February and everything was still going well but then the bombshell hit in my personal life that knocked the stuffing out of me. Sunday morning 7am my sister Siobhan rang and she was crying on the phone. She said: '*Skin, there's something wrong with Da*'. I told her not to panic and I jumped out of bed and would be at Da's house ten minutes later. When I got there an ambulance was outside and I thought great, at least we won't have to wait and waste time if it is serious. My brother Tony is an ambulance co-ordinator at present and has worked as an ambulance driver most of his life so he was on the ball today. I hurried inside and my neighbours Joe Maher and his wife and Christy Dunne and his wife were standing in the sitting-room. I walked past and said: 'Well, Christy, what's the story?' Chris never answered me as at the same time Siobhan came down from the room and threw her arms around me saying: *Oh Skin, Oh Skin he's gone!*

Tony then met me and said: 'Fuck it, I thought we nearly had him back' and he was angry having carried out CPR for a good while on Da but unfortunately he didn't make it. I went to Da's bedside and held his face in my hands and he was still warm. I never thought for one second following Siobhan's call that Da would be gone when I got there. I just thought he was unwell and would go to hospital etc. for treatment. To this day it breaks my heart that I never got to say goodbye and the night before I went to ring him about 10.30pm having heard on the news that Kieran Fallon would be the new jockey for the Coolmore operation and that Jamie Spencer was finished there. I remember saying to Vera I may tell Dad the news but then I said: 'Ah, I'll tell him tomorrow as he might be in bed.' It still pulls on my heartstrings that I didn't. My poor Mam sat the opposite side of the bed and cried uncontrollably and both of us held Da's face until it turned cold at which point Mam held my hand as both of us sensed the cold of death at the same time.

It was a terrible time and being such a large family there were people arriving by the minute as the sad news spread. My poor sister Mary was in Scotland that morning and had to be given the news over the phone from my brother Frank. I was asked to ring my brother Mick and it was a horrible feeling having to say over the phone that my Da was dead, to my brother. I apologised to Mick for having to tell him by phone when he called to the house an hour later. I then rang Vera and she knew straight away by me. I sat into my car and turned on the radio and I distinctly remember U2's song written by Bono for his Dad who had died was playing and it will always remind me of that horrible day in the words of: '*Sometimes you can't make it on your own*'. Da was laid to rest later that week in St. Michaels and I visit his grave nearly every Sunday morning and make sure the grass is always cut etc. It's the least I can do for the man I loved to bits who was not just my Da but my mentor and best friend. God rest you Da xx!

Losing someone dear is one way of making you take a step back and having a look at yourself and how you live your life etc. It helps you realise what is important in life and what your priorities should be. My Da always said that life is too short to enjoy every minute of it cause you could be dead in the morning. I had every intention of giving it my best shot and trying to own a winner in the sport which my father loved would be an even greater quest for me having lost the man.

I was supposed to call to see Penny that same sad Sunday but she would be the last thing on my mind for a while as I struggled with the thought of not having my Da around never seeing him again. I went back to work after a week or so and took each day as it came. All the lads from *Going Forward* were a great support and before long a couple of us went to see Penny to see how she was progressing. She was improving no end and laid-back attitude for such a big filly was a great sense of comfort to me if that makes any sense to you. I loved that horse and it was thought she knew I was sad as she rubbed her head against my stomach when I held her. I remember thinking that Da would be looking down on her for me.

The following month Penny went into full training with Mick on the Curragh and in May we got our first chance to see her do a fast canter on the *Old Vic Gallop* which runs along the side of the Curragh racecourse. It was really special for me to see our own horse flash past on one of the most famous gallops in the world with one of the most famous jockeys ever to sit on a horse, in Johnny Murtagh. We were in the big time! I remember giving Johnny a lift back to his car in the back of mine and being such a huge fan of his, this was my first claim to fame in racing. Mick was very pleased with her work and said she was on course for her first run sometime in July or thereabouts. She was so big that it would take a while to get her even close to full fitness.

Well as I've said before the months flew past and before we knew it July was upon us and Mick entered Penny up for her first race in Navan racecourse, Co. Meath. I was not gonna be there as I had booked a two-week holiday in Turkey during the same time. I didn't mind missing the race as Mick had told me she was only 60% fit and the race was just to bring her on a bit. Don't worry if she finished last as she probably will, he told me. I made sure to tell the syndicate members the same thing word-for-word. Jay stayed at home while we were away and Hec collected him the morning of the race and together they went to watch Penny's debut. He text me that day to tell me that Hec brought him for lunch on the way and as they sat in the restaurant the song: 'Penny and Me' came on the radio. Hec said it was an omen. Penny did finish last that day under Rory Cleary but nobody was disappointed as it was the first step. Three weeks later she ran in Navan again and this time she finished fifth in a five-furlong maiden and was running on nicely at the end. It was encouraging to say the least.

Her next race entry was for Fairyhouse and luckily enough she got into the race so we all decided to have a summer evening out and watch Penny together for the first time. There was great excitement all round and we thought she might have a slight chance of being placed. It was a very hot summer's evening and a beautiful evening for racing. Penny ran in I think the third race on the card and was priced around 16/1. We all had a few bob each-way from the account just from the heart so to speak. She was right up with the pace from the start and the commentator mentioned her name lots of times. It was a six-furlong maiden and at the two-furlong pole she was cruising. Just as they were asked to quicken Penny got an awful bump from the horse next to her who tried to work her way out from the rails. It completely knocked her off her stride and our jockey Emmet Butterly did well to stay on. Emmet got her straightened up and she started to go well again and would you believe it got bumped again. God help her she tried to come back again and was flying at the finish but the post came too soon. She finished fifth again but this time was only two lengths off the winner and a head-and-neck and neck behind the other three. I have no doubt that with a clear run she would have at least been in the first two, may have even won. I didn't know whether to laugh or cry to be honest but at least we had a half-decent horse going forward so the syndicate name was working out well. Penny had only two more runs that season as a two-year old by which time the weather had become miserably wet and in soft ground she was never going to be at her best. She did run respectably in her last run in the Curragh however so we put her away for the winter in Valerie's. We were pleased enough but cursed the weather for changing just as she was at her peak. That's racing for you! You just need everything to go well on the day. By the way, during this season Penny's full brother had actually won twice as a three-year old so we were all over the moon in the hope that she might do it for us next year.

She was back in Mick's the following February and her three-year old campaign would begin in earnest that summer. Before this however, Jay, Marc and I were awaiting a very special event around April time. Curtsey was due to give birth to our eagerly awaited

Kalanisi foal. It's hard to keep up with the racing and breeding lark. Curtsey having gone over her time with her first foal had us guessing would she do the same again. This time however she was to take us by surprise completely. The lads had monitored her very carefully as usual and were happy enough that nothing would happen maybe until early May. Punchestown racing National Hunt festival was on the last week in April and Marc and Jay decided to go on the day of the Irish Champion Hurdle. I was working and didn't bother and Curtsey was out in the paddock during the day so they'd keep a check on her each night she came in.

That day however at approx. 3.30 in the afternoon Jay rang me in a bit of a panic. '*Da, where are you?*' 'Eh hello, Jay, I'm in work, like'. '*The mare is after foaling*'. 'What mare?' '*Curtsey ya eejit!*' 'She's not due for a few weeks'. '*Tell her that*'. 'You may go home and catch her quick'. '*Catch her? What the hell are you on about? She had the foal in the field, Da - and Granddad can't catch her*'. 'Oh shite, right I'm gone, is it a colt or a filly?' '*I can't see from here - helloo!*'. 'Oh, good luck I'll ring you when I'm home'. '*Grand, we're on our way also*'. Ninety miles an hour to Athy from Newbridge.

When I eventually got to the stud farm Eamon was standing at the gate with a bucket of oats calling Curtsey who was miles away galloping around like a mad horse with the foal galloping alongside and *she* not even three hours old. The afterbirth was still hanging from the mare and she was in a right state. I walked towards them saying: '*Woh the girl*' '*Woh the girl*' '*Come on Pet, come on*'. Proper horsey talk, eh?? The two of them just flew past me. How in the name of Jaysus was I going to catch her?? I tried ten times and eventually I cornered them and Marc and Jay arrived just as I did. Jay took the rope from me and got it on Curtsey and I had my arm around the foal's neck as she followed her mother. We got them to the stable and had a good look at the foal. 'Not a bad foal Marc, but another filly' says I. 'Ah yeah' says Marc, 'but she is a nice one'. 'Lucky she didn't damage herself' says Jay. We all agreed but it was a lot easier for us than the last time, I said. 'Thank God for that' said the two lads together.

Anyway there she was, our little Kalanisi. 'Nice foal' said Eamon, 'but ye could have done with a colt this time lads, but sure there's nothing you can do about that'. 'You'd never know, if Kalanisi is any good as a sire you'll get just as much for a filly if she's very correct' says I, me being the expert at this stage. 'You could be right, Skin' says Marc and at that we left them alone to get to know each other. We had no trouble whatsoever with this foal and she was out in the field for months soon after. She was a lovely little foal even though she wasn't very big. Jay went to see her a few times every week and I think he was half-afraid to become too attached to this one following what happened the Soviet Star. We had already decided on the next stallion for Curtsey's third foal. He was a son of the all-conquering stallion *Danehill* and we would bring her for covering the following week. I said to the lads that I think we should sell this one as a foal to get some money back in at this stage and they both agreed that come the time we'd put the reserve at €15k to cover the cost of Kalanisi worse-case scenario. It would be a few months away but no harm to have a plan in place and right now I had a share in three horses and it was more than enough when it came to the bills.

I was now dabbling in horses in some sort of way for nearly three years now and the only money I was seeing was all going the wrong way - *out!* Not that my good wife ever reminded me of this or anything!!!

I needed this to be my year. In my quest to own a winner I would have settled for a good return on the foal at this stage of the game to be close enough to owning a winner. Time would tell.

Penny was back in and I think she may have had an introductory run to her three-year old campaign but in July of that year Mick rang me to say we were running her in Galway. I said: 'you mean *the* Galway' and he said yes, she runs on the Monday evening in the 7.35 race and Johnny will ride. 'Johnny *Murtagh?*' 'Yes', he said. 'That's great, Mick, thanks, I'll be talking to you before then'. The Galway Races are a huge event in the Irish racing calendar and to have a runner in the Galway Festival is a huge honour for any owner. I rang Hec and said we're off to Galway and he said: 'Go way ya fuckin' luder!' his words. I said: 'I swear to God Mick just rang me a few minutes ago'. 'Kelly, you must think I'm an awful *eejit*'. I had to ask him to wait and I called Jay to the phone. 'Will you tell that gobshite that I'm not pulling his leg, Jay?' 'Howya, Hec' said Jay, 'it's the truth, she's off to Galway for the handicap on the first night'. 'Jaysus that's great news, sure we'll have a bit of craic down there so. Right Skin, I'll tell the others so and we'll round up the troops, are you going down to Galway for the week-end? The *Sawdoctors* are playing in Eyre Square on Sunday'. Hec, I'm only after finding out she's running and you want the itinerary for the week already, give me a chance to think about it *like!*' 'Right so' he says. 'well, I don't know about you but I'm goin' anyway' and he hung up. This sort of banter is what being involved with a racehorse is all about and to have winner would just be the cherry on top. Mind you a winner with my luck so far was still a dream. I remember a funny little story at home one night with something my Nick said. Vera had asked me when was I gonna get a few bob back from the horses. I said I didn't know but I was driving a 01 Citroen C5 at the time and had it four or five years and I jokingly said that I'd buy a new car when the horse starts winning. Straight away Erica said: 'Daddy, there is no way that Citroen will stay going for another thirty years!' And they all had a right laugh at it. I called her a cheeky little fecker but had to laugh as well.

The Galway Races

If you've never been to Galway city during race-week you just don't know what you're missing. The place is just alive with people and music. Café bars, restaurants, pubs you name it, they are all full and everybody in good form. Traditional Irish music sessions crop up everywhere and the craic is mighty. Add to all of this the beach and amusements of the gorgeous *Salthill* and ask yourself what more could you ask for. Well maybe a full week of horseracing at the local Ballybrit track for the annual Galway racing festival and now you have all you need for a week of laughter and song and the ups and downs of a hectic week.

We decided to go there on the Sunday morning just Vera and I. Jay and Hec would travel down on Monday to be there for Penny's race that evening as would some of the other syndicate members. My sister Mary and her husband Johnny Pender also travelled on the Sunday with some friends. It takes about two-and-half hours to reach Galway from our home and we arrived there around mid day. We parked up the car in our B&B which was very nice and we had a nice short walk into town where later in the day The Sawdoctors would put on a free show for the thousands gathered in Eyre Square. We had a bite to eat and relaxed in the pleasant Galway sunshine waiting for the band to appear. They came around 3pm and played right through to 5 and we sang along to 'The N17' and 'I used to love her' and many more besides. It was a super day out and just the tonic for the day ahead tomorrow. Mary rang me and we arranged to meet up with them in the bar of their hotel later that night. BAD MISTAKE. We had a drink and headed back to the B&B for a lie-down followed by a shower and back out to meet with P.J.Digan and his wife Sheila, Sheila's brother John and his wife Kathleen. Johnny and Mary came in a few minutes later. Unexpectedly then Siobhan and my other brother-in-law Steven arrived. We were all in good form and the slagging over Penny was only beginning. P.J. and Johnny were calling me *JP* for the evening as in millionaire Irish horse-owner *JP McManus*. 'I wish', says I.

Well the drinks were flying in as is always the case when P.J.'s in the house. He is a very close friend of the family and is one of the nicest people I have ever met. Some man to buy drink though. As soon as the glass is half-empty he has one on the way. All very well till the next day but on this occasion I felt the adrenalin would overcome the hangover. *Yeah right!!* A couple of lads with guitar and banjo suddenly arrived and that was that. We fell out of the place around 3am with me having sang my heart out for hours and Mary having told everyone in the place that 'Penny and Me' was a *certainty* for the following evening. Isn't drink wonderful? Vera and I eventually got to the B&B having staggered the whole way. Next morning I awoke with my tongue stuck to the roof of my mouth and with a headache that would kill a horse. The young foreign girl in the B&B showed us to the breakfast table and within minutes she served up a full Irish, set for a king. I devoured it and felt much better afterwards. Two *solpadeine* and a bottle of water and I was ready for the day ahead. The lady from the B&B asked us were we going racing and I said yeah, we have a runner there tonight. 'Oh, my God' she said: 'wait till I get a pen and paper' to write down the tip, as she called it. 'I can tell all my friends I got it from the owner' says she. I thought to myself that they probably already heard it following Mary's performance last night. 'Penny and Me, isn't that a lovely name!' 'Don't have too much on' I told her and off we headed first to Salthill and then to visit a friend of mine from Athy who moved to live in Moycullen just on the outskirts of Galway city, Conleth Dooley. Con brought us to his lovely home and treated us to tea and sandwiches and we had a good old chat. He thought it was wonderful to have the horse running in the Galway festival and asked me if she was any good. I told him I'd know around 7.45pm that evening. We stayed longer than we maybe should have in Con's place and were cutting it fine to get back and change etc. and get to Ballybrit as the traffic would be crazy. Crazy was an understatement as it took us so long to get back into the city that we had no option but to head straight to the track and change into the gladrags in the car.

Just as we drove into the racecourse carpark it began to spill rain. An almighty torrential downpour and apart from anything else I couldn't help but think that such heavy rain was not what Penny needed. 'Ah well, nothing we can do about that now' says Vera. 'They'll all have to run on the same ground'. I never laughed as much as the two us tried to change in that car. The rain was so heavy I couldn't even let a window down and with the windows all fogged up,

Vera in her bra and knickers and me in my boxers we just couldn't talk for the laughing. I kept thinking people will think we're up to something and kept saying to Vera that all we need now is the RTE cameras to show a shot of the car park. Eventually we were dressed and had to wait about twenty minutes for the rain to ease at which stage we made a dash for it.

We met up inside with Hec, Jason and his friend (Jason also) as the two Jays were staying down for the week. Hec had torn his good suit jacket and was like a hoor over it. I wouldn't mind but I told him it wasn't even noticeable but sure I may as well have been talking to the wall. Siobhan, Mary, Steve and Johnny then all arrived along with P.J. & Co. Stephanie and her husband who were syndicate members were also there. We had a nice little crowd and the craic was good in anticipation of what lay ahead. I of course was a bag of nerves and couldn't have a drink as I'd to drive home later due to work commitments. However if Penny finished first three, that might change.

Mick had phoned me earlier that morning to say that Penny had travelled down well from Kildare to Galway and he was hoping she'd run well as her work was quite good leading up to the race. I told all the members and all we could do was hope for the best. The place was absolutely packed with people as it always is and I said to Hec how nice it must feel to have a winner in front of so many. Penny would run in the fourth race 7.35 and at around 7.15 my legs were like jelly. I had met lots of people from home and they all shouted 'Best of luck, Skinner' to which I replied: 'I'll need it all!' to each of them.

When we entered the parade ring Tracey Piggott, RTE's racing correspondent asked Mick, who was with us, if he would give a pre-race interview on Penny's chances. All the women in our group were fixing the hairs and make-up etc. as they were in the immediate background on live TV as were the rest of us. Johnny Pender was in his element. Mick said the same to Tracey as he'd earlier said to me and that he was hopeful of a good run from her. There was also an interview with bookmaker Sean Graham and with Brian Gleeson of RTE and would you believe they both gave Penny as their idea of the winner. The pressure was on.

Johnny Murtagh then arrived in our red-and-white colours and put his arm around me and said 'Right Bren this is it!' and he was full of laughs and jokes as to how nervous I was. I asked Vera to take a photo of Johnny and I and it still takes pride of place at home. I wished Johnny luck not that he would need it with his experience and so it was all down to Penny from here. We all had a good few bob each-way and were hopeful. We remained in the parade ring with Mick to watch the race unfold on the big screen. The rain had stopped by now and it was a pleasant evening. Penny was in stall number 8 right in the middle and within minutes Des Scahill announced 'And they're off!'

I knew after about one hundred yards that Penny's action in running was all over the place and that she wasn't enjoying it. I was hoping that Johnny might be able to perform a miracle and get her travelling sweeter. Galway is a very undulating track with sharp bends and it is common knowledge in racing that some horses love it and others hate it. Some are even-course specialists and can only win there. For a brief moment Penny seemed to improve but alas I knew she was not gonna fall into the Galway specialist category this evening. Johnny tried everything in his power but she never got into her stride at all. She came in seventh, which was disappointing and I knew by Mick that he was expecting much better. I'm of the opinion that the earlier rain ruined our chances though we all had our own reasons. We knew she was better than that and that's what made it so disappointing. Mick said to us that he was sorry but we didn't blame him and it was back to square one as to where we'd go next. Penny was fine after the race so who knows maybe she just wasn't good enough but that's racing. As I said before you just need everything right on the night which isn't always easy to have. I thought about the long drive home and I let a few *fucks* out of me as did the others and shortly afterwards we went our separate ways. I was extremely quiet on the way home and Vera asked if I was ok. I remember saying to her that I had just received one of the biggest kicks in the bollox to date in my life. That just about summed up the evening. We stopped for something to eat and a few hours later we were home. Hec drove home alone, having dropped the two Jays there for the week and he rang me about 12pm to say 'That was *cat*, wasn't it?' so I told him to go to bed and I'd talk to him tomorrow. Mary stayed for a few more days and had to hide for fear of her drunk prediction.

A few weeks later would you believe Penny ran and in Galway again just at a standard meeting. Johnny, Mary and my brother Paddy travelled down to represent us as none of us could make it for one reason or another. I watched the race with Vera in a bookie's office in Newbridge en route to Dublin airport to collect Erica who was arriving in from a three-month working trip to Australia. Penny ran much better this time but still finished ninth but behind a wall of horses who literally passed the line together in a remarkably close contest. Penny was only three lengths off the winner but I was still without the elusive first winner. She would later run her last race as a three-year old in the

Curragh but again I'm afraid no luck. What do I have to do was my swan-song for yet another season. Penny's full brother won three times again that same season including a premier handicap with prize money of €100,000 on Derby day in the Curragh just to rub salt in my wounds. It is difficult to keep a syndicate together with as much money involved each month and nothing but hard luck stories.

Decision Time

Penny went back to Valerie's again for the autumn/winter. We decided to sit down before the beginning of the next season to decide on her future. Valerie did have a trainer's licence and we asked her if she would be interested in giving it a go with Penny as a four-year old. It would reduce our costs significantly as Val's was a much smaller operation than Mick's with less overheads etc. I rang Mick and he agreed we should give Val a go with her and that Penny cold be a stable star for her. He said if she ever wins he would be first to congratulate me and wished me all the luck in the world. I thanked him for all his effort and wished him all the best for the future. The syndicate agreed that Penny would spend her four-year old campaign at Valerie's and this would be her last year if she didn't win.

Round about this time I still had the Kalanisi of course whom in the interim we had brought to and from the yearling sales which turned out to be another weak sale in which we were only offered silly money for her in. She was ready for pre-training now also so I had this to sort out on top of the decision with Penny. Marc was involved with a lot of horses from the stud at the time and asked me to take ownership of the Kalanisi between Jay and I and maybe try her for a few runs to see if she might be the one. Easier said than done in such an expensive game. My brother Aidan who worked and lived in Dublin had asked me if I had any shares available in a horse as a friend of his was interested in becoming involved. I told him about the Kalanisi and he arranged for his friend John to meet me and have a look. John met me one Saturday morning in the Standhouse Hotel at the Curragh racecourse and I brought him over to Valerie's after we had a coffee and a look at her pedigree. John knew a bit about horses and was already involved in another syndicate who had a winner at one stage. Having viewed the filly he said he'd like to have a share and that his friend Dave may like to do the same. Dave was to come down the following Wednesday which he did and he also bought into a piece of her having seen her in the stable while it absolutely bucketed down rain outside. A friend of mine in work, Mark Kane, also from Dublin had heard me talking about this new syndicate and I also brought Mark to see her. Mark was quick to make me aware that he wouldn't know the front from the back of a horse but thought she was a little beaut which I suppose she is. He also became involved and *Quattro Racing Syndicate* was born. Time to start filling in forms and choosing colours not to mention names again. I had asked Valerie if she was interested in becoming her trainer also and thought Penny would be the ideal type to have working with her and it also meant I got the best training fee possible having two in at the same time. Will I ever get sense was the overriding thought in the back of my mind.

A Chuisle mo Chroi

Picking a name for the Kalanisi was one hell of a lot easier than had been the case for Penny and Me. The film *Million Dollar Baby* was in cinemas at the time and I thought this was a great name for a horse and I suggested it to each of the lads. They thought it was a great name also so I enquired if it was available. Unfortunately it wasn't so we had to think again. In the film the female boxer was affectionately known as *Mo Chuisle* which is a Gaelic term for 'My Darling' or 'my Pulse'. This would be our second choice, but it was gone also. Sticking to the same theme we thought of 'A Chuisle mo Chroi' which is Gaelic for 'The Darling or the Pulse of my heart' and so the Kalanisi became the darling of my heart and would be named *A Chuisle mo Chroi*. We asked Valerie to kick off training her and we hoped she would be a nice early type to run as two-year old. I now had two monthly bills and all of the headaches of two H.R.I. accounts. Was I mad?? YES I was but all in the quest of owning a winner. Penny and Me and A Chuisle mo Chroi my last throw of the dice or else – divorce.

Both horses did well during the winter months although *A Chuisle* was a fussy little eater by times which bugged me a little as if a horse is not eating up well there is something somewhere amiss. However she had plenty of time as Valerie was patient with her and coaxed her along to have her ready for the following flat season. In fact both of them were ready to run around April/May of that season. We had a few entries in April for both but much to my frustration each time we were balloted out and didn't get to run. In May we tried again and A Chuisle would run in a two-year old maiden in Roscommon and Penny would kick off her four-year old campaign in Limerick in a competitive handicap.

Mark and I travelled to Roscommon to see A Chuisle as John and Dave couldn't make it as it was a mid-week race. This particular summer was absolutely deplorable weatherwise and the ground in Roscommon was bottomless. Rory Cleary, a young up-and-coming jockey based in Mick's yard took the ride for us. Rory knew her well as he often rode her work coming up to race entry stage to see if he thought she was ready. Because of the dreadful soft ground we asked Rory or should I say Val asked just to give her a nice bit of experience in a fifteen-runner field and bring her back safe and in one piece. Rory did exactly this and A Chuisle cam home in twelfth, believe it or not and I was delighted as she was my first runner who had not finished last in her first attempt. Clutching at straws or *what*, says you!!

Penny went to Limerick the following week and had worked brilliant at home prior to the race. We were fairly confident of a first-three finish but the Friday night before the race on Saturday it rained all night. I remember Jay saying to me 'Da, I think the man above is trying to tell you something'. I believed him. How and ever it was off to Limerick regardless the following day. Penny was now in the best form of her life and looked it. She was strong after the winter grub and fit from both experience and her home work. Unfortunately four others in the race were fitter and would you believe she finished fifth again. What the hell was it with her and fifth?? She was only a head behind for fourth which would have got her and us a few bob prize money. Still with the ground against her it was a very good run. In the coming weeks (still raining by the way) six horses from that race, including four who had finished behind us actually won races. Jaysus it must be my turn soon. We entered Penny for a race in Tralee Co. Kerry and she was accepted. Great plans were made for us all to travel for the weekend to this beautiful part of Ireland and I swear I knew in my heart and soul that this was it. The horse was ready, the race was right up her street and Hec had the B&B booked so everything was in place. Well almost everything!! All I needed now was for Martin King TV3 weatherman to put a sunshine symbol over the Co. Kerry area of the map but would you believe it he put up the dirtiest big black cloud with huge raindrops on it that he had in his collection. Rain between the showers was the forecast. I rang Tralee racecourse during the week and a nice man said to me over the phone 'Son, if you think anything of your filly don't run her here this week it's like a bog' in his best Kerry accent. That was the end of that as I rang Valerie and we decided there and then to pull her out of the race due to conditions. I then had to ring Hec first of all to cancel the accommodation arranged and booked and then the others. I could sense everyone was pissed off of the whole thing and I could see why. I was in the very same boat. The joys of owning racehorses. I thought of a man once telling me that the only way to become a millionaire with horses was to start out as a multi-millionaire. Think about it!!!

A Chuisle did not like the soft ground either so for a few weeks there was nothing we could do. Where I worked in Newbridge there was lots of interest in racing and I was not the only one with syndicates on the go. A few close friends of mine also had their own and were just as frustrated as I was. The lads such as Brian O'Sullivan, Pat Abbey, Leo Taaffe and Frank Kenny were more drawn towards the National Hunt side of racing and Pat in particular was always telling me 'Skin, whatever chance you have over the jumps you're at nothing trying to compete with the big boys on the flat'. Typical of me of course if there's a choice between the hard and easy way to do anything I'd always go for the challenge. Mind you I would've settled for a donkey derby at this stage. I said this my cousin Pe Dunne one night and he replied 'You have to stay at it, Skin, remember every long journey begins with a small step'. I told Pe that I thought I may have taken the wrong direction however and he just laughed.

The lads from work had been down the same road as me however and were now on the second horse each hoping to strike gold. They had all the same stories to tell such as soft ground, hard ground, stiff competition, balloting systems, money and bills, and in their case bad jumping or being boxed in at a crucial stage in a race. One of the syndicates had a half-decent horse at one stage who was second once and third another time only to get sick for a while and after being nursed back to health he went and badly damaged tendons in his comeback race which ended his racing career. Another of the syndicates had a filly with a top National Hunt trainer who had showed promise early on only to burst a blood vessel in a race and was out for a full year as a result. She later came back with a smaller trainer and ran badly a few times but clicked recently in her own handicap grade and finished third. It then ran again and finished ninth instead of going the other way, maybe second or first even. The lads and I would often spend hours discussing just how difficult it was to get the winner and I often said in those conversations that if it ever happens me I was booking into a rehab clinic for a month as I'd be on the beer for three months prior. We still have these chats and again it's all part and parcel of the sport and not knowing if any of us will ever experience the thrill of a winner in a way keeps us going. Only recently one of the lads was telling me that he was getting so much grief from the wife over the horse that he didn't tell her that the horse was running the night it finished third and only remembered he hadn't told her when he started shouting out the horses name near the finish, as he watched her on telly. She wasn't long about letting him have an earful even after the horse ran well but as he said, if the horse had run shite she never would have known so he wasn't sure what he was hoping for in his own words. I could just picture him though with his imaginary whip as she fought out the finish. Hopefully the lads will have their day sometime also.

One thing you must have if you have a horse running in your name is thick skin. The slagging from friends, workmates, family is unreal. Then there's the odd begrudger who is delighted to see your horse finish last or well down the field. Thankfully I only have one of the latter type and to be honest he's just miserable anyway. The day after the horse would run he'd be there waiting for me with his whingy voice 'I see the horse ran well again yesterday' he would say sounding like '*Nyin nyin nyin* horse *nyin nyin* yesterday' to which I'd always reply 'Ah, go fuck yourself'. He was the type of fella who wanted more money for everything he did in the job and was the laziest fucker in Ireland. You know the type!! If I ever do have a winner, I'll go looking for him.

As for the rest of them well it was something one had to take in good spirit, otherwise there would have been murder. Some of the comments I could do nothing else but laugh at anyway such as

'Well Skin, how'd she get on yesterday?'

'She was 12th'

'I was wondering why I couldn't see her but the wide lens on the racing channel wouldn't have even seen her at that'.

'Funny aren't ya' was all I could say.

Or 'I saw your horse running last night Skin, you should've backed her each-way as I think she went the other way'.

'If they'd went around twice, she would have won by half the track' was another. I remember telling another close friend early in play that I'd love to get my name on the *Irish Field*, the superb weekly edition on Irish racing. I have it left by in Paddy Donoghues newsagents and pick it up every Saturday without fail. On the top right-hand corner Paddy always writes 'Skin Kelly' in case he's not there and the assistant will find it easier for me when I go in. I had it in work with me one Saturday morning and left it on the stores counter as I helped the lads serving a good few at one time. The aforementioned friend went to read the headlines and instantly shouted to the audience 'Be Jaysus, lads, he finally did it, he got his name on the Irish Field', pointing to where Paddy had written it. I could have killed him as mr miserable was there at the time and said 'it's the only way he'll ever have it on it' or rather '*nyin nyin nyin nyin nyin*'. Can you just imagine how nice it would be to get a winner and be able to say 'up yours' to all of these slaggin' bastards. All good fun though, I must say. My mother and brothers and sisters would watch out for them running so I also had to listen to the likes of 'What the hell are you at with them horses?'

'Can you not see you're pissing against the wind?'

Or my poor mother trying to be nice 'She did her best, Skin, but I don't think she's good enough'.

'I think you could be right, Mam' was all I could say.

It rained for ten whole weeks this summer. I thought it would never stop and we even considered sending the horses to England for a run but I couldn't justify the expense of it all unless the horse was an out-and-out certainty to win. Unfortunately I could not be this confident either so we just waited for the rain to stop. And waited and waited.

Eventually it did pick up a bit again and even though the ground was far from perfect we needed to get a run into the horses just to keep them fit and ready if nothing else. Peny was accepted for a run in Down Royal and the ground came close enough to just right for her. This course is up north and a long way for us to travel so none of us went although we did think that she had a good chance in the race. It was her handicap grade and even though she was without a run for a while she was still doing lots at home and doing it well. It was a Friday evening and the 6pm start to the race was perfect for us to watch on 'At the Races' channel at home. Valerie had two in the race and at the time Penny was working far better of the two on their homework. Rory took the ride on Penny which I was delighted about as I think he's a super little jockey.

For some reason, this evening I was not nervous at all and thought this race is there for the taking' so here's hoping. Penny looked brilliant on the night with a full shine on her coat and was fit as a flea. She had a reasonable draw in the race and the seven furlongs was spot on for her. She jumped away nicely and was well-positioned at the first bend but then all of a sudden Rory dropped her right out of the race for some reason. Something was amiss and I thought 'Well what this time?!' She pulled up and just trotted back in. Valerie rang me straight away from the parade ring on Penny's return. 'Sorry Bren, she has burst a blood vessel'. There was blood in her nose and on Rory's silks which told the story straight away. I told Val that I'd chat to her when she had time but for now Penny was out of training and as far as I was concerned this would be her final race. Each of the syndicate members rang me and I explained what had happened and we decided there and then to take Penny out of training as I was afraid of this happening again unless she took a long time out and none of us were prepared to wait a year while still paying monthly bills for vets etc. Penny would not run again and would be brought to the breeding sales a couple of months later it was decided. Val kept her for me at minimum costs until then. There was great disappointment all round. Val's other horse finished 4th in the race and knowing Penny was better than her at the time only served to sicken my arse completely. A couple of months later we brought Penny to the sales and sold her to a college friend of Jason's who was going to breed a few foals from her and enjoy having her around the place for riding out etc. Best of luck with her, Michael, I hope she breeds you a derby winner. I genuinely thought Penny would be my first winner but no, the quest continues and now with just the one, A Chuisle, the baby we had reared from birth. The only good thing about Penny gone was one less bill coming in the door.

A Chuisle was entered for a few races and balloted out of most which was frustrating having waited for the rain to stop prior to this. She was eventually accepted for a run in Sligo where it had been raining and Val was not too keen on running her. We were so pissed off at this point that we said 'let her take her chance' more out of frustration than anything. Stupid mistake. A Chuisle could hardly stand up in the bog-like conditions and was pulled up along with a few others in the race thanks to the sensible jockey on board that night. What a waste of time and money. With horses you need the patience of a saint. From there on I left it with Valerie to say when A Chuisle would run.

So with a long, wet summer, one less horse and a totally pissed-off remaining syndicate this was one miserable season. A Chuisle would run once more this term in a 2-year old maiden of thirty runners in the Curragh on the last day of the flat. She ran just about ok and we put her away for the winter.

During the winter months I must say that I enjoyed the hassle-free environment of not having to ask the lads for money and watch entries and numbers for balloting etc. If I'm completely honest I have to say I was tempted not to bother my arse anymore. All the money spent, all the nagging, all the advice, all the slagging, all the excuses, all the ifs and buts, it just wasn't enjoyable anymore. I thought about it for weeks and discussed it with the lads and they all felt the same. We had from November to February to decide so we said we'll leave it until February and if we still feel the same we would sell A Chuisle and call it a day.

For years I managed underage gaelic football for my home town of Athy. I would train the lads each Tuesday and Thursday night and have a game most Sunday mornings in the Minor (Under 18s) league and later in the Championship series. This was a passion of mine for at least ten years as when I was younger I absolutely loved the game and was quite a good player. However when I was 19 I cracked a vertebrae in my back and this put an end to my GAA career. Later after various treatments I was able to play soccer and did so for years with my beloved Athy Town FC seconds and I had a few tremendously enjoyable years with them. Managing the minors in the GAA suited my work schedules however and for years I ran up and down sidelines shouting at referees and players alike with my good friends Gerry Delahunt, Colm Reynolds, Ned Martin and Jimmy Kelly.

I thought if I gave up the ownership side of horses in other words if I got sense I could go back to managing the football or maybe even take up golf with a few of my brothers who had been playing for years and were fairly decent golfers at this stage. I watched Jay play in a county minor semi-final which they lost in the last second and should never have lost and I thought I may go back to the football as this gave me a great urge to go one better with the lads the following year. I drove myself mad deciding what to do as a pastime as doing the lawns at home which I was quite good at sounded more like a retirement move right now.

I see Hec regularly through work and he often said to me that he was glad to be away from the whole frustration of mostly the entries farce of Irish Racing and I must agree that when I went into owning horses I had never allowed for this side of the game. It is a very complex situation and I don't really want to get into it right now. The governing body are currently trying to reduce the numbers by eliminating horses who go below a handicap rating of 45 which will help but my own personal opinion is that they should also increase the number of races at the same time. Ireland recently unveiled its' first all-weather track in Dundalk and to be frank it's about bloody time. We are world leaders in thoroughbred racing and breeding and to have only one all-weather facility in this day and age is ridiculous. The Curragh, which is HQ of Irish flat racing is crying out for an all-weather track in my opinion and they are currently spending millions in making the Curragh a state-of-the-art facility and rightly so, but this does not include an all-weather track as far as I am aware. On top of this the Dundalk track was closed for most of last winter. What is the point of having an all-weather track if it has to close at any stage of the year. After all I thought 'All-Weather' meant racing in all weathers thus extending the season, meaning more opportunities for owners to get a run for their horses. An all-weather in the Curragh plus the one in Dundalk opened all year is the way forward in my book even if it means reducing prize money in winter months to help pay the extra overheads or else increased sponsorship from the big companies who do well out of racing, for instance. Entering a horse up to four or five times in an ordinary race and being placed on lists of 50 to 60 and sometimes even more entries for a 14 to 15 runner race is just not acceptable anymore and if not sorted will indeed kill off the lifeblood of Irish racing. It still takes all the hard work and extra time to have a horse ready to run and then to find out only days before the race that you are balloted out is soul-destroying for the owner. It is also soul-destroying for the trainer but at least they still get paid for the month regardless. I know the trainers want their horses running but it is definitely the owner who gets hit hardest. Anyway it's not up to me to sort out but I can still give an opinion. If anybody comes back and tells me that if your horse is good enough they'll get plenty of runs I'll tell them where to go as the fact of the matter is that there will always be lower-grade horses in the mix and it's only fair to give them every opportunity to run as often as they are ready to do so to either go up or down the handicap and well and good if they go too far down well then they're out. If we only cater for the big guns in racing it will results in five and six-runner events in the Curragh etc. and see how many patrons will bother paying twenty euros minimum to watch these.

This brings me on to another side of racing which annoys me by times. Bear in mind I write this not because I'm just some old cranky, mean-arse who just wants to give out. I write this from the heart because I just so happen to love horseracing. The fall-off in attendances at Irish race meetings is there for all to see. I'm not referring here to the likes of the Galway or Punchestown or Irish Derby festivals, I'm talking about the bread & butter meetings week in, week out. I don't just mean down the country either. I include classic days at HQ even. I have been to all 1000 and 2000 Guineas days for years and in recent years the numbers have rapidly decreased and would only compare to a mediocre evening meeting in the UK. I've been to Naas, Leopardstown, Gowran Park and Cork for cards which included listed and group events and again the crowds are below average. Why is this?? It is easy to point out all the bad points in any form of life but I'd prefer to try be pro-active and see what can be done. I know some efforts are being made to attract people back and that the development of the Curragh will be state-of-the-art but will it mean doubling the entry fee or a large hike of some description to the ordinary punter. If it does it will get the crowds for a while until the novelty wears off.

In my opinion the whole secret to getting people back is promotion, promotion, promotion. Get the people inside the gates for free for midweek meetings and at weekends ensure there are top-value family tickets available. Increase the numbers inside and with levies from Tote and bookmakers increased as a result, it can off-write the small amounts currently paid at the gate as a result of the current small numbers attending. Add to this the monies spent in the food and drinks areas and this also helps. Mind you this area needs reviewing as why should I pay more for a pint, a lot more for a burger & chips for the kids just because I'm at the races?? Promote these products correctly also and the increased volumes at reasonable prices will more than compensate for fall-offs in profits today. If I want to bring my wife and kids (both adults) to the races it will cost me €80 before I get in. If we have a couple of drinks and something ordinary to eat it is another €60 at today's racing prices and we don't back a winner speculating four €5 bets (optional) per race on a six-race card that's another €120. Add these together and it is €265 for an ordinary day at the races. I'd get two weeks in Spain for two for that money!! Or damn near it. Is it any wonder people don't go racing like they used to?? Ah well that's just my opinion anyway and hopefully something positive will happen in the not too distant future to put Irish racing days back to where they should be.

What's another year?

Now that I've got all my frustrations off my chest it is back to the drawing board and deciding what to do. Do I take the easy way out and go back to the football? Do I play a few rounds of golf with the lads? Do I just start going racing again as a neutral and start enjoying it again without all of the bills and all of the excuses etc? I'll give the lads a shout and see what vibes I get from them. John was first and he was of the opinion that A Chuisle was only a very young horse and we should at least go another year as a three-year old and see has she trained on. When I told him he owed the account a good few bob it was a bit of a different story but in fairness to him after he cursed and blinded for a few minutes he said go for it. 'If we sell her for half-nothing and some other bollox gets her to start winning I'd shoot you Skin'. That's John sorted. Dave next.

'What do you wanna do, Dave?'

'Oh Jaysus, here we go again' he says. 'What do you think?'

'It has to be your decision, Dave'.

'Jaysus, you're a great help!'

'Well, if it's any benefit to you, John wants to keep her in as a three-year old!'

'Ah Skin, I think he's right as it would do my head in if we sold her for some other bollox to start winning with'.

Who's this other bollox everyone's on about, I thought to myself.

'Yes, I know what you mean, Dave, I've just had the same conversation with John almost word for word'.

'What does Valerie think? Will we leave her there with Val?'

'All Val can tell us is that the filly does show potential at home, Dave, but you know and I know that we get nothing for finishing first up the Old Vic. If we do put her in with someone else we will have a much bigger monthly bill and the same horse. As far as I'm concerned if she's good enough, Val is well up to getting a win from her just the same as any top trainer would be.'

'Yeah, that's true. We may try another season but if she doesn't win or be placed she can go off show-jumping or something'.

That's Dave sorted. Mark next.

'What do you wanna do, Mark?'

'What do you mean, what do I want to do?'

'About the horse, Mark, do we keep her in training for another year or will we sell and cut our losses.'

'Why do you ask?'

'Because I have to, Mark. I have to get money from you every month again if she stays in.'

'Sure what's different about that?'

Holy divine, I'm pissin' against the wind here.

'I'm just saying, Mark, that now that the new season is getting close, that I need agreement from everybody before I decide.'

'Well, why did you not just say that then?'

Oh, holy divine!!

'Well, I know nothing about horses, Bren, but isn't she only three this year?'

'Eh, yes, your point?'

'My point is she's only a baby so why do you want to give up and maybe see her win for some other bollox?'

Here's your man again.

'I know, Mark, but I just have to be sure that we all agree before I give Val the go-ahead to kick on with her'.

'Well, I think we'd be stone-mad not to, don't you?'

'Yes, I do, to be honest, but I had to have your decision from you and not just from me.'

'I'm after telling you I think we'd be mad not to stay going?'

'Alright, don't ate me. So you want to stay in so?'

'Yes, how many times do I have to tell you? Yes, count me in. What's another year, says Johnny Logan!

Mark sorted, so what can I do now but go with them as after all this is all my doing.

'Hello Valerie, I spoke to the lads and they all want to try her as a three-year old'.

'No problem, Skin, sure you'd have to imagine if some other bollox bought her and she did the business for him'.

Lord Jaysus, did the three lads meet with Valerie prior to me ringing them all??

'Right so, Val, how is she anyway?'

'She's ok, but I'd like to see her eating a bit more than she is'.

'Is she eating up at all?'

'Ah yeah, but nothing like she needs to'.

'What do we do?'

'I've tried a few different type foods and had her checked over as all we can do is hope for the best'.

Fair enough!

So after all this the quest for a winner is down to an under-nourished three-year old name 'A Chuisle mo Chroi'. Could she be the darling of my heart and against all the odds be the one to do it for me. Deep down I must admit that my confidence levels of ever owning a share in a winner are now at an all-time low and I'm thinking with my luck to date anything will be a bonus at this point. I sat down with Jay one night at home and asked for an honest opinion from the maestro.

'Da, to be perfectly honest, I think that Kalanisi might turn out to be more of a National Hunt sire. We probably shouldn't have even run the filly until she was four and go the jumping route with her'.

'Well, says I to myself 'what makes you think this?'

'A four year-old hurdler by the name of *Katchit*, Da' was Jay's reply.

Katchit, a son of Kalanisi had just spent his first year jumping hurdles in the UK and was becoming something of a revelation. A tiny little horse who was winning lots of races, some of a very high calibre. Katchit had run plenty of times on the flat prior to this but with no success. I said 'Oh yeah, but that doesn't mean that all of his off-spring will do the same and that the dam side of the breeding has to come into it also'.

Jay said 'I know, but I'm just going by facts. Kalanisi has another four year-old called *European Dream* and he's also won over hurdles this year, he also won on the flat as well I know, and the way Katchit is going he could be a live contender for the Champion Hurdle next year. Mark my word, Da, if Kalanisi breeds a five year old Champion

Hurdle winner from his first crop he will be a National Hunt sire this time next year'.

My Jay know his horses and I said ' that's all very well, but what do we do? She can't jump until she's four, she might not take to it even then so do we kick on with her on the flat this year?'

Jay says 'You may keep her going, but I don't think she'll ever win on the flat for us, Da, she's always going to be caught for pace if deep-down her breeding is for two-and-a-half miles National Hunt-pace type races. You may just keep her going without being too hard on her this year'. Interesting, to say the least!

Anything I take on long-term I always like to have some sort of plan and indeed a plan B if possible. I had various discussions with the lads and all agreed that what Jay said had made a lot of sense but the facts of the matter are that to keep a horse in training for a year would cost approx. €14k so we had to ask ourselves what was the best way forward from a practical and financial point of view. We decided to let her take her chance on the flat and let's play it by ear and see how she goes. In May of this year, A Chuisle was still fussy enough with her food and Val tried everything with her. I was tempted to bring her to McDonalds at one stage. Even so and though physically there was nothing of her in it she was still doing all her work and doing it as well as could be expected and had a nice shine on her coat and had passed any veterinary inspections so we had no choice but to kick on and enter her for her next race.

Here we go again with the entry jungle. We entered her four times before we finally got into a race in Ballinrobe, Co. Mayo. The entries we missed out on were all close to home of course, but had ridiculously high entry numbers. Ninety-six, seventy-three and sixty-eight I remember. Crazy stuff, but I've already been there. Regardless we were now off to Ballinrobe for a one-mile, two-furlong three-year old maiden. Of course a few of the big yards were represented so it was fingers crossed for A Chuisle's first run of the season. It was a Tuesday evening so none of us could make the three-hour spin from Kildare/Dublin to Mayo. There were fourteen runners and we were hoping for her first run that she would finish well up in the first ten at least. Shane Gorey was aboard this time so again we had a very good pilot. When they jumped away, Shane kept her right up with the pace and it was encouraging that she was well able to do so. To make a long story short she ran very well and finished in my now familiar fifth position. She was a good bit behind the winner but Shane was of the opinion that there might be a day out for her in the future. 'Nothing wrong with that run, Da', Jay says to me after the race and that was good enough for me. Each of the lads were happy enough as was Valerie who said she would keep an eye out for a nice handicap race for her and if there was none forthcoming we might try another maiden. Unfortunately you can't just pick out your next race on the calendar as you must go through the entry saga before knowing where you run next.

A few more entries!! Missed out on the handicaps which she was eligible to enter for and eventually had to settle for a fairly competitive maiden in Navan. We were lucky to get Shane again and most of us travelled to Navan to see her in the flesh. She acted up big-time in the parade ring and got herself into a right old state which worried me a little to say the least. When she got to the stalls there was no way she was having any of it and Shane used all of his horsemanship and experience to keep her in toe. The stall handlers eventually had to put a hood on her to coax her into the stalls. At last she was in but I was thinking that all of this would go against her in the race which indeed it did, but mind you under the circumstances she ran OK on ground she did not like also. However when she got back to the stabling area she was found to be heavy in season which explained everything. Shane was disappointed after the good vibe he got in Ballinrobe but because of the fact that she was in season we just had to discount the race. My wife however loves what she calls 'all of these excuses' and was straight up in her criticisms about what was it going to be next time?? Fair point, but what can I do if nature decides to take its' course the same night I decide to take her to the races?? Anyway, still no winner.

Vera, my wife, also mentioned on numerous occasions that I should've learned from my experience with a greyhound a year or so prior to me becoming involved with horses. She was referring to an undertaking I became involved in with my great friend Tom Bride. Tom was mad into the dogs. He had trained a few greyhounds in England when he lived there but when he moved back home to Athy he had a longing to buy 'a good dog, one good dog'. I can still hear him saying it. 'Skinner Kelly, one good dog is all we need'. I told him I'd go half with him and he could manage the whole thing after a feed of Guinness I hasten to add, in Ger Clancy's bar in Athy one night. I thought no more about it for a few weeks when one night Tom (*Slam* is his nickname) rang me out of the blue to say 'Skinner Kelly, I found the dog'. I thought he was after finding a greyhound on the side of the road, the way he said it.

'Anyway Slam, tell me more about it' I said.

'A bitch in Derrinturn near Edenderry town has eight of them and we have the pick.'

'That's a terrible thing to call the woman, Slam' says I.

'The bitch is the *mother*, you eejit!' says he 'and she's a multiple winning *bitch*. I know the lad who owns her and he said we can have the pick of the litter'.

'Oh, right now, I have ya, Slam. Hey, what kind of money are we talking about here' I asked him, thinking maybe £150 apiece or so.

'The male pups which we want one of are one thousand pounds each but he'll let me have one for eight-fifty' says he.

'She must be some bitch, Slam' says I.

'How much were you expecting to pay, Skin?'

I said about £300.

'*Three hundred*, for jaysus sake, you wouldn't buy a fuckin' *Jack Russell* for that' says he.

We had a laugh and decided to go see the pup on Sunday.

I drove over on Sunday and a man and his son brought us to the kennel and there was eight greyhound pups jumping all over the place and we standing in the middle of them. The owner was big into greyhound breeding and brought us into his sitting room to show us videos of the bitch winning a few decent races. If one of them is half as good as her he'll make a super stud dog after racing, he said. I knew nothing about greyhounds but Tom would fill me in on the way home. If the male dog was any good at racing he could be used as a stud dog for a fairly sizeable fee thereafter. We decided on a nice frintle-coloured dog before we left and paid for him there and then. The man would keep him until he was ready to go into training a few months later. Slam was thinking of a name all the way home. Tom's son Danny came to Athy having been reared in England with an '*Awight* Skinner *maite*, how r u *todie* then'-type Cockney accent but after a few months in

Athy he went to the other extreme with a kind of '*Howya* getting *an*, Skin' slang. Tom always said Danny's gone '*Rail Fla*' the way he talks. 'That's it, Slam' says I, we'll know the dog affectionately as 'Rail Fla' until we name him properly when he runs. Rail Fla grew into a superb-looking greyhound over the months and was with a pre-trainer somewhere in Kildare. The week before he was to join a top dog trainer however, we got some bad news. The previous Sunday Tom had told me that Rail Fla was flying on the training fields of coursing or whatever is the proper term is, but this time Tom called to tell me that Rail Fla had broken his leg and had to be put down after a trial run in which of course he absolutely flew. Should I have given up on my quest for any type of winner back then?? Maybe I should've bought the fuckin' Jack Russell Tom eluded to earlier. Ah well, he may never have made the track but he gave Slam and I hours of endless greyhound chats and hopes for the future when we did have him. Rail Fla, may he rest in peace.

We brought A Chuisle home from Navan and Val let her have a while off before we got her going again and the old reliable Irish summer decided to arrive around the same time. Rain, rain and more rain. Dundalk all-weather facility had just been opened around this time and I was really keen for A Chuisle to take her chance here so Val was asked to enter her up any chance she got. She entered her for a few mile-four handicaps and eventually she was accepted for one. All weather racing in Dundalk was on Friday nights and A Chuisle would run in the last at 9.40pm. I was really anxious as to how she would do as she was used to doing most of her work on this type of surface. She was well in herself at the time and it was great to get her a run here. Unfortunately with the race being on so late none of us could make it and once again thanks to Sky Television and 'At the Races' channel we were able to watch it live at home.

By the time 9.40pm came around I was of the opinion that it may be past A Chuisle's bed-time. It was certainly getting close to mine as I had a very early start the next day. They showed her in the parade ring on telly and she was on her toes once again and I prayed she didn't start acting up and have her race run before it even started. Luckily this time she settled down fairly well and went into the stalls after two efforts by the handlers. The pace on the all-weather can be faster than the turf and this was definitely the case tonight. However, A Chuisle was loving every step of it and was third and going nicely the whole way around. Two furlongs out with Colm O'Donoghue in the saddle, she is right with them and it's time for me to start roaring at the telly.

'*Come on, my little chicken*'.

(That's what I've always called her affectionately) and she was still there in third on the outside. All of a sudden she almost stops and it was obvious that Colm knew there was something wrong. I couldn't understand it and thought blood vessel burst as did with Penny, but all I knew is that I was devastated as she was definitely going to finish in the money for the first time ever and may even have won. I waited for Val's call. Before the race, Vera had asked Jay and Erica 'What's the excuse gonna be tonight?' Boxed in, bad draw, burst blood vessel, jockey made a stones of it . She had them all as she'd heard them all from me, unfortunately. My phone rang.

'Were you watching?' asked Val's voice.

'I was, of course, what's the story?'

Are you ready for this? Here's a new one for Vera's collection.

'She swallowed her tongue' says Val, 'and she was gonna be first or second, I'm sure of it. She was flying when it happened'.

'Ah, fuck that anyway, Val' I said 'go on, I'll talk to you tomorrow'.

I put down the phone and told Vera and the kids. All they could do was laugh at the latest excuse to be honest but did say what a pity as she did look like winning for a second. I lit a cigarette outside in the garden, I walked around calmly talking to myself and thought 'What in the name of *Jaysus* do I have to do to get a winner??' This is definitely the final straw. I spoke to each of the lads and like me they couldn't believe it but to a certain degree they were delighted she had ran so well and was ok. I don't know anymore, says I. I lit another cigarette, spoke to myself for a while again. First sign of madness, I thought although I was thinking that maybe trying to own a winner won the first sign of madness category hands down.

I came back inside and Jay said 'I don't think it's meant to be, Da'.

I said 'I think you're right, Jay' and made a cup of tea and decided to have an early night. I said goodnight and Erica said:

'Sleep well, Da, careful you don't swallow your tongue!'

The slagging had already begun. What could I say?? I twisted and turned all night thinking how could I be so unlucky.

Only Fools and Horses

The next morning I went to work at 6am and even at that early hour 'Nyin nyin' was waiting for me. 'What happened her this time?'

'If you must know, she swallowed her tongue and one more word out of you and I'll make sure you swallow yours'.

Strangely enough, he said no more. I went up to the canteen for a cuppa to start the day and I met a good friend of mine who had watched the race the previous night.

'I saw your horse running last night, Skin, were you disappointed?'

'Ah yeah, I thought she was gonna be placed, John, and all of a sudden she pulled up' and I explained the reason.

'There's always some excuse with horses, Skin, too many things can go wrong'.

He continued and we both began comparing trying to own a winner and trying to make money backing horses and came to the conclusion that horses are a mug's game and that they make fools out of intelligent people. John had lost a few bob on the horses the previous night and wasn't in the best of form as a result. We finished our tea and asked ourselves simultaneously:

'Will we give them up, though?'

'Yeah, right, we will in our arse'.

Horses can become an addiction and I don't make light of this subject as gambling on horseracing has ruined many lives but in my case the addiction has been for the love of horses and horseracing. I'm not saying I haven't lost or won on them by times but the stories and the fun of the game are the parts I am addicted to. Jay and I are also addicted to the whole breeding side of the sport so between reading up on them, having a bet on them and trying to own a good one of them is it any wonder I'm nearly gone mad. Having said all of that where would I be without them? Some of the best laughs I have had in my life have been in a bookie's office or at the finishing post on a racetrack.

I have often walked into our local bookies to the sound of grown men shouting obscenities at a TV screen.

'Go on, ya fucker ya!'

'Let him on you stupid bollox'.

Or if they are having a good day, you might hear;

'Go on, Johnny, ya little daisy! - he was a stupid bollox the day before'.

The different emotions at the racecourse are similar where you have those who backed the winner jumping up and down while those who lost calling all the fuckers under the sun.

Then you have the 'tips'. All straight from the horse's mouth, of course. I'm sure it's the same all over Ireland, but in Kildare (the Thorougbred County) the tips are as regular as the weather reports. I love the way some lads give a tip. They whisper or say 'Not a word to anyone, right?' and then tell at least fifty more the same tip and those fifty in turn tell another fifty each and so it goes on and on. The problem sometimes is that there are tips for four of five horses in the same race which rightly messes up your calculations, so the only advice I can offer is to pick your own horses and hope for the best. Mind you, there have been times when the information is spot on and there's nothing nicer when a group of people go for it and take a nice few bob from the bookies. What's seldom is wonderful.

I remember a funny story in the bookie office in Athy one day where a local man name Mickey had a tip for a horse in one of the later races on the card but had lost a lot of money in the earlier races. In an effort to come out on top he had a very large bet on the tip. He took a price of 16 to 1 and if the horse won he stood to win a substantial amount. He had all his money on the nose meaning the horse had to win for him to collect. He told us all the name of the horse and also told us how much he had on and how badly he needed him to win. We all had a few bob on and the shop became like a scene from a movie as we all waited in anticipation for the race to begin.

Just before the race began a local middle-aged woman Mrs. Whelan who loved to have small bets just for the excitement came in and had ten pence on a different horse at odds of 5 to 1 in the same race as Mickey's tip. It was a jumps race over two-and-a-half miles with about twelve fences to jump. Richard Dunwoody was riding Mickey's tip and Adrian McGuire was riding Mrs. Whelan's selection. The race began and you could have cut the tension with a knife. Mrs. Whelan was a great woman to shout and get very excited right from the start of the race. Mickey on the other hand was white in the face with fear. The race was beginning to take shape and all the time Mrs. Whelan shouted 'Go on, McGuire' 'Go on, McGuire' repeatedly. From the second-last fence it developed into a two-horse race, Mickey's and Mrs. Whelan's of course.

'Go on, McGuire!' 'Go on, McGuire, ya have it!'

As they came to the last it was neck and neck and Mrs. Whelan was jumping up and down making hand signals and at this stage roaring:

'GO ON McGUIRE, GO ON!'

at which stage Mickey found his tongue and roared:

'GO ON DUNWOODY, YA HOOR YA!'

'GO ON, McGUIRE'.

'GO ON, DUNWOODY'.

Coming up to the finish, Mrs. Whelan let out a tremendous roar:

'GO ON McGUIRE, YA HAVE IT!!!'

To which Mickey replied:

'SHUT UP to be fucked, Mrs. Whelan, if your horse loses, I'LL pay you'.

Jesus, the shop erupted with laughter and when Mickey's horse passed the post a nose in front, he threw his arms around Mrs. Whelan and said:

'Fair play to you Missus, I owe you fifty pence'.

She congratulated Mickey and said 'I never enjoyed a race as much'.

'I nearly had a fuckin' heart attack watchin' it' Mickey replied.

It had been so exciting that the rest of us almost forgot that we actually backed Mickey's tip. I'll never forget those few minutes as long as I live.

Then there's the story of Johnny Murphy and Mrs. Riley. Johnny was a young fella who worked for a small trainer who rented the stables at Fortbarrington some years ago. Johnny did everything from cleaning out to riding work to grooming and keeping the yard and tack room etc. clean and tidy. As is the case with lots of small trainers in Ireland they were competing against stiff competition and finding it extremely difficult to come up with one good enough to win a race.

I spoke to Johnny regularly and each time he mentioned that if anything it was becoming even more difficult by the day. That was until Mrs. Riley came along. Mrs. Riley by the way was not a woman but rather a small little well-bred filly and according to Johnny the next time I spoke to him she was passing out the pigeons on the gallops during the morning workouts. 'Skin, I swear to God she is like a fuckin' little rocket' Johnny's words.

He minded Mrs. Riley like a child for weeks, maybe even months in getting her ready for her next run. She had ran twice before but Johnny was now adamant that the penny had now dropped with her as to what racing was all about. Every morning at the crack of dawn Johnny prepared Mrs. Riley for her morning workout. Even though nobody was watching, Johnny brushed her and cleaned her hooves and had her looking like she was about to run in one of the top classic races. It was obvious to me that Johnny had fallen in love with this little filly.

I met Johnny a few weeks after he told me about the pigeons and he ran over to me and told me that the day had finally come, that Mrs. Riley was to run in Sligo the following Tuesday evening.

'I'm telling ya, Skin, whatever few bob you can get your hands on, have the whole lot on her'.

'I hope you're not letting your heart rule your head, Johnny' I told him and he said:

'No way, I'm not codding ya, Skin, me arms are nearly two inches longer just from trying to hold her on the gallops'.

'Well, I hope she wins for ya, Johnny and I mean that from the bottom of my heart' I told him.

'I fuckin' hope so, Skin, 'cause I'm havin' me wages on her'.

As it turns out I had to call to Fortbarrington on the Tuesday of the race. It was early morning, about 8am and when I got there the lads were loading Mrs. Riley into the box and heading off on the four-hour spin to Sligo. I noticed when Johnny walked her into the box that Alan the trainer closed the door and walked to the jeep. I asked him was he not forgetting to let Johnny out?

'Skin' he says, 'Johnny insists on travelling in the box with the horse in case anything happens to her.'

I stood at the back of the box and asked Johnny was he alright in there? He had a few bales of straw between him and Mrs. Riley and another bale behind these for him to sit on.

'I'm grand, Skin, not a fuckin' bother, nothing's gonna go wrong with my baby today' was his reply.

I said 'Johnny, do you realise Sligo is four hours away?'

'I don't give a fuck' says Johnny, 'me and the Mrs. Are off to make a few bob together'.

I couldn't help but notice the shine from Mrs. Riley's coat as Johnny had looked after her so well that he had her looking like a million dollars. I wished them luck and off they went. As I walked away I said a quick prayer to myself that everything would go well for Johnny and the Mrs. The poor little fucker deserved it after all his efforts.

The reason I was in Fortbarrington so early that morning was because we had some English visitors home and I was bringing them off for the day. We drove to Wicklow for the day and showed them lots of different beautiful scenery in this lovely county. We spent hours in Glendalough and walked for miles through forests which overlooked the magical lakes below. It was a glorious day and when we got back to the tiny village I brought them for scones and jam in one of the many cottages which specialised in the art of making the perfect scone not to mention the pot of tea. I have never seen people enjoy scones and tea as much in all my born days and they still talk about it years later. I think that the fact that we walked nearly ten miles up and down hills and in and out through trees beforehand may have been the reason that they enjoyed them so much as they were bloody starving and would have eaten anything that was put in front of them anyway.

I then brought them towards the coast and before long we were in Arklow where we stopped off and spent some time on the beach. It was about 4pm in the afternoon and all of a sudden it dawned on me that Mrs. Riley's race was at 5:30pm so I asked everyone to relax on the beach, that I had to go down town for a minute. I found a small little bookie office and asked the girl behind the counter if she could give me a price for Mrs. Riley in the 5:30 in Sligo. She was a contrary aul' fucker and snarled at me:

'Who's Mrs. Riley riding?'

'Mrs. Riley is the horse' says I.

'Stupid name for a horse' she says.

Very pleasant woman, I thought to myself.

'I've no price on Mrs. Riley anyway' she says, so I said:

'Here, I'll have twenty quid on her anyway'.

'What time do you close at?' I asked.

'5' o clock' she replied.

'That's not much use to me' I said nicely to her 'if the horse wins'.

'I didn't ask you to come in here to back it' she says, so I said 'Fair enough so' and I walked out and found another bookies where I had ten pounds each way on Mrs. Riley at odds of 25 to 1. The man in the office asked me where I was from and when I said Athy, he said they had a shop in Carlow if I wasn't around to collect should the horse win, so I could collect it there which was close to home. The race wasn't televised so I headed back to the beach. We stayed a while longer and headed for home, having had a lovely day. We stopped in Tullow, Co.Carlow and had bite to eat and when we got back to Athy we went for a drink in Smuggler's bar. It turned into a major session so lots of friends arrived and the drink was flyin' and a few verses were attempted. We eventually went back to the house in Fortbarrington and had a few more drinks and a sing-song till about 3am. It was time to go as I couldn't drink or sing anymore for tiredness so we walked out to the car to head home.

I'd had such craic that evening that I had forgotten completely about Mrs. Riley's race. One of the lads who doesn't drink was turning the car in the driveway as we approached. He did is best to get the drunken ones into the car and it must have taken him a half-hour to get going. He pulled out of the yard and as he drove away he noticed a yard light in his rear-view mirror and he asked me should that light be on all night or should we go back and see did the lads leave it on by mistake. We turned around and went back and two of us went down the yard to check if all was ok. Halfway down the yard, I noticed that Johnny was in the stable with Mrs. Riley and he was being a bit forceful putting a night rug on her and he was kind of cursing to himself. I put my head over the door and couldn't wait to hear how she got on.

'Well, Johnny, how did she run?' I asked.

'Jesus, Skin, you frightened the *shite* out of me' says Johnny.

'How did she run' says he, 'she ran like fuckin hairy goat.

I didn't know whether to laugh or cry to be honest with the way he said it.

'Ah, maybe next time' I said, in an effort to console him.

'She can fuck off with herself now' says Johnny 'and as for those *fuckin'* pigeons, I'll shoot the slow *bastards* in the mornin'.

I bursted out to laugh at the way he was feeling and Johnny could only do the same. I put my arm around him as he walked out and said:

'That's horses for you, Johnny'.

'I know', says he 'the bastards would put ya out the door'.

I remember telling Eamonn the next day what Johnny had said and he nearly died laughing. Many years later we often tell Johnny's story over a pint or two and it really is the stuff which past stories are made of. 'She ran like fuckin hairy goat' and 'The slow *bastard* pigeons'. Classic!

Being from a large family with such varying ages, each of us have all met some wonderful characters down the years and when we do get together at weddings or parties etc. I think it's fair to say that there are so many stories and jokes to be told that we've often had pains in our stomachs on the way home for the laughing.

My brother Mick for instance, has a story for all occasions. He is now fairly bald as is his best friend Bill. One day he and Bill went to the local barbers for a trim on the bits they had left and shortly after they'd left their friend Hughie came into the barbers for a haircut. The barber said to Hugh that he'd just missed Mick and Bill to which Hugh replied: 'What the *fuck* were they doing in here, selling *tickets?*' Mick tells this story on a regular basis, normally before he starts slagging me over the horses finishing down the field, but always in good faith.

Mick, Tony and I grew up together as there is just two years between Tony and I and Mick is one year older than Tony. I was always the young lad of the three and as a result I got away with murder. I remember the two lads *mitching* from school and bringing me with them, (not that I wanted to go or anything) and when they were eventually found out, my Dad gave them a right earful and never said a word to me. However after the twins Ger and Aidan, who are four years younger than me, came along, then I was the one getting all the earfuls while they got away as the little saints. I'm sure it was the same for Eddie, Har, twins John and Mary, followed by Francis and Paddy, then Mick, Tony, myself, followed by the other twins Ger and Aidan, then David the youngest lad who was never in trouble as he had always one of us to blame followed by Siobhan, the youngest of us all, who was not just the apple of Da's eye, but the apple of all of our eyes being the little girl, the youngest after all the lads, not forgetting Mary, of course. You have to be very careful in our house not to exclude anybody!! Seeing all of those names written on one page makes me realise how grateful we should all be to our Mam and Dad that we were all so well looked after all our lives, regardless of numbers. There is also a great sense of comfort for me in seeing that at least Da got to see us all grow up before we lost him. Is it any wonder that there are so many stories with so many names?

When we were growing up Mam bought all the weekly groceries in Purcell's which was a pub and grocery shop situated beside the canal bridge just in front of the Asbestos (Tegral) factory. Purcell's today is a public house and our local and Paddy's second home, as previously mentioned. We used to take turns at collecting groceries for Mam. Three of us would often jump up on the bike. Tony would pedal, Mick would sit on the cross-bar and steer and I'd be on the handlebars holding on for dear life, especially on the return journey with three or four bags of shopping consisting of sliced pans, bottles of milk, sugar and the likes. The main reason we never minded was first of all it was great sport especially in the dark when Mick might steer into the ditch or a pothole or the likes and secondly because we always asked Mr. or Mrs. Purcells for *Ten Carrolls* cigarettes. So there we were, three young lads having a right smoke for the two-mile journey home. We always made sure to tell Mrs. Purcell to put the fags down on the weekly bill as a half-pound of butter or a box of cornflakes or something. Now and then she forgot (on purpose I reckon) and holy jaysus our Da went stone mad.

'I'm not working hard all week for yee three little fuckers to be smoking, it's hard enough to feed yee, never mind keep yee in fags and by Jesus, if I ever catch any of yee with a fag in your mouth, I'll shove it down your neck, *lighting*'. We used to wait a few weeks after the bollocking before we bought another half-pound of butter on the bill. Da never really smoked, but Eddie thought he looked like James Dean with a fag in his mouth and he was the culprit for the rest of us trying it on and off. I'm still trying to give the bloody things up today and wish I'd never started. It is now common knowledge that smoking can kill you but when we weren't killed off that bike and when Da found out we were smoking I reckon we have a good chance of surviving for another while. Before Tony, Mick and I started going for the few messages to Purcells, Eddie, Harry and John and so on used go so I'm sure they had the same fun and probably the same bike come to think of it.

My Da didn't get his first car until most of us were nearly reared. How the hell could he, says you! When he did, however, the craic was 90. A yellowy/mustard Fiat 124, 'JIR 59'. Francis picked it out for him in Midnight Mickey's local garage. Fair play to you, Fran. It was probably the worst car, actually no, it *was* the worst car every made. It broke down more often than a lame horse. I can remember being called out of my bed in the early hours of the morning to give Da a push with the heap of shite so that he could make it in time for the 8 to 4 shift.

One day I'll never forget, Da asked us to come in to the factory car park, take the battery out of the car and leave it up to Loughman's garage to be charged up. He said collect it in the afternoon and put it back in the car for when he came out. The three amigos on the bike called in, took the battery out and I carried it on my lap on the crossbar and we smoked all the way out to Loughman's. Sean asked us to collect it at 3.30pm and off we went. When we went back at 3.30, Sean was very busy and didn't get to give us the battery until about 4.15pm. No mobile phones back then to ring Da to tell him we were delayed, we went as hard as Tony could pedal on the bike back to the factory in town. When we got to the car park the three of us nearly fell of the bike with laughter as there in front of our eyes was Da, sitting in the driver's seat of JIR 59 with about ten lads pushing the car trying to get it started. Mick walked over with the battery in his hands and called the lads to say 'Lads, I don't think she'll start without this'. Well, the ten lads together shouted: 'Har Kelly, ya fuckin' *eejit*, we're nearly dead pushing this yoke and you knowing there was no battery in it!' Da stood out and all he could do was laugh and then apologise. 'What the hell kept yee three ?' he said, with a huge grin on his face. He put in the battery threw the bike in the boot and the four of us laughed the whole way home.

You're probably wondering at this point about the horses!! Well, as I write, it is summer time in Ireland, which means rain, rain and more rain, whatever the hell is going on. Some horses love to run in soft ground and can be at their very best so some owners and trainers pray for the rain as a result. I wish to Jesus they would ease off a bit on the prayers at this stage as this filly of ours (A Chuisle) just does not act on soft ground. Mind you, she has no academy awards on good ground either to date, but whatever hope we have she'll never run well on the soft.

Following the tongue-swallowing episode in Dundalk, we entered A Chuisle into a race in Downpatrick, which is in the north of Ireland. We genuinely felt it was her best chance to run into a place (finish in the first three) as she really was flying in Dundalk and a repeat of that run minus the tongue-swallow would be good enough to get her involved in the business end of the race. None of us travelled to the racecourse as it was a bit far away and we were all busy in work so we decided to have a few bob each way in bookies and watch it on *At the Races*.

I remember watching the earlier races and noticed that they were not using starting stalls for some reason. I was concerned about this as A Chuisle is inclined to get a little bit excited at the start as you know and therefore to ensure a level break I really wanted the stalls to be available. Too late now, however, as it was time to cross the fingers and toes and anything else I could cross. The instructions to the jockey were to get her up near the front from the start. The starter asked the jockeys to walk around in a circle for a few minutes and as they straightened up he would let them go. A Chuisle was being her normal self and was on her toes throwing the head up and down, so I was a bundle of nerves. Just as she came around in front, the starter shouted 'Ok, lads' and was just about to shout 'Go!' when one or two horses strayed a bit to the side so at the last second he shouts 'Whoa! Whoa! Hold on' and asked them to circle again. I let a few curses at the telly as she had been perfectly positioned to kick off in front. Around they go again and as A chuisle went to walk along the rails one of the other horses shyed in front of her and A Chuisle took a few steps backwards and would you believe it as she did the starter shouted 'Right Lads, off you go!' She was left about six lengths behind by the time she took off and I was livid. That was it, not a hope in hell of her passing enough horses from behind. It is just the way some horses are, they either go from the front or they just don't run to their full potential. What a bloody waste of time and money. She passed four or five as they slowed up but she finished way down the field, so needless to say it was frustrating. I really felt like throwing in the towel there and then. Valerie rang me and was every bit as disappointed as I was. I gave the lads a call and we decided to give it a couple of weeks before we made up our minds as to what we would do with her.

Jay had always been adamant with me that Kalanisi's had turned out to be more of a National Hunt sire and this was backed up particularly by the performances of *Katchit* and who against all odds won the Champion Hurdle in Cheltenham, which Jay had predicted would be the case. As we all had the thinking caps on at this stage it was time for firm decisions to be made. Because of A Chuisle's poor placings she had fallen down in the handicap ratings to 43 which would rule her out of running on the flat again as this is the current means of reducing the numbers for balloting which I happen to agree with. So it was a case of running her over the jumps or selling her off. Because of her breeding, we said wouldn't it be just our luck to give her away and for some other owner to win a hurdle race with her! We asked Valerie if she would school her over a few hurdles to see if she could actually jump and we'd take it from there. Val said she might be worth a try, so that was the plan.

I don't know what the hell it is with me and horses but I hasten to add that I don't let my heart rule my head when it comes to keep on trying. It is indeed the quest to own a winner after all the hard luck stories that keeps me wanting to go on. Don't ask me to explain. Maybe I'm just mad, I don't know.

Henry

My brother Tony and his wife Martha have four kids today. They are Tara, Anthony, Shane and the youngest lad Henry. Henry is called after my Da and the main reason he is, apart from being Da's grandson is because when Henry was born, he had so many complications that it is a miracle that he survived at all. I admire the chap so much that I couldn't even begin to tell you how much. He has spent most of his life in and out of hospitals with all sorts of problems such as heart and lung illness. He needs an oxygen tent while sleeping, could not attend school for fear of infections, cannot enjoy his food because of throat problems, has spent days and nights over the years in intensive care units not knowing if he would pull through, but yet he is 21 this year and still always manages a smile or a joke everytime I see him. He has never been able to participate in sports such as football, soccer or whatever, but rather than sit around the house all day, whether he feels well or not he decided to become involved with, would you believe? Horses. I wonder where he ever got that from!! Tony has always dabbled in some form of horses over the years so in order to allow Henry to have his interest become possible,

Tony sold his house in the town and bought a few acres a few years ago on which he built a few stables and a couple of paddocks and himself and Henry now run a small breeding operation in connemara ponies. It's definitely a safer option than the one I chose of thoroughbred racing but regardless of money or costs , I think the genuine love of horses has given this young man great comfort and enjoyment not to mention the will to keep going. Horses have a funny way of making some people eat, drink and sleep horses. Henry is forever on the mobile phone talking to fellow breeders. He is forever on the road to Clifden, Co. Galway with Tony to show ponies in the hope of coming up with a champion one day. Anytime I visit he is out straight away to go through the current crop in the stables and his eyes light up as he goes through the details of each one by one. Her mother is such-a-one and her father is this one etc. Henry is the Connemara pony expert, just as my Jay is the thoroughbred version. Henry was at my nephew Paul's wedding with us all recently and had just found out the wonderful news that he is now on the list for heart and lung transplant in Ireland, which is a huge, huge step in his young life as up until now he has never been strong enough or in a position to even consider same. Tony was telling me how pleased they all were at this news but when I spoke to Henry he never even mentioned it as all he wanted to talk to me about was horses. Priorities eh!! Well, Hen, all I can say is you're an inspiration to us all and long may we talk about horses.

Miss Minnies

My youngest brother David, who happens to be as fond of horseracing as I am, decided to go the same route as myself and bought a nice filly through one of Ireland's up-and-coming young trainers David Myerscough. David rang me one Thursday evening and asked if Jay and I would meet him in Ragusa Stud farm on the following Saturday morning to have a look at this yearling filly by a stallion named *Fram* as he wanted our opinion. I asked him was he sure he wanted our opinion based on our luck to date.

He said 'Yes, go on, you might bring me a bit of luck'.

'Fair enough' says I, 'but at the end of the day, don't blame me if we make the wrong decision'.

Saturday morning bright and early, Jay and I headed off to Newbridge as the experts to give our opinion. Two right experts says you!! A CV which includes a greyhound who broke his leg, a yearling who broke her pelvis and three horses on the track to date who could not get past fifth position in any race and who had performed dismally to date. However God loves a trier and in fairness he must have been very fond of us at this stage.

We met Dave in Newbridge and travelled in his car to the stud farm. It was a bitterly cold morning and I remember asking Dave was he mad and would we all not be better off tucked up in our warm beds at home? He just laughed and said 'To hell with it, if we don't chance our arms we'll never break our necks'. Where had I heard those words before, I thought to myself? When we got to the stud farm it was an absolute gorgeous place with some cattle and sheep grazing in the paddocks mixed with a few mares and yearlings out for a few hours in the freedom of the pleasant surroundings.

The young trainer met us and showed us around. It was obvious to us that he took great pride in both the facility and the horses he began to show us. We walked from stable to stable viewing some really nice horses of all ages until eventually he said 'Now, in here is the one you are here to see'. I couldn't wait to see what she looked like. Jay had spent months in Fortbarrington with the new crop of yearlings there and was very anxious to compare this one with them. The young filly was half-asleep when she was led out for us to have a look and I'm sure she must have been wondering what do these lads want at this hour of the morning!

Well, there she was. A nicely-made little filly with a lovely temperament and I have to say she caught my eye straight away. Jay viewed her inside-out and upside-down as she walked along and thought she was very nice but was a bit concerned about the sire's success to-date with two-year old runners etc. We spent about an hour viewing the filly and David told the young trainer that he would decide in the next few days as to whether or not the filly would be his. Goffs yearling sales were taking place the following week so Jay was of the opinion that maybe he should have a look at a few there prior to making his mind up. The filly we viewed was priced at €26,500 and had been bought from the Doncaster sales in the UK by the trainer to sell on to a new owner. What Jay was saying made a lot of sense as it was quite a lot of money to spend on the first horse Dave had seen.

'What do you think, Skin?' Dave asked me.

I told him that I thought she was very nice and that maybe it might be wise to see a few in Goffs before he decided. I then said to him that at the same time I think if you don't buy her that it could come back to haunt you. He thought for about two minutes and next thing he just said:

'You're right, Skin, I'm gonna buy her'.

'Don't blame me if she's useless' says I.

That was that. Dave said he'd give it a couple of days but his mind was made up. During the middle of the following week he rang me to say that he was now the proud owner of a Fram filly and I wished him luck and said I hope she wins a group one for you. It was a brave decision on his behalf to take the chance on the first one he had considered.

The plan from there on was for the filly to stay with the trainer and he would let her grow for a few months before he would break her in and prepare her for training for the following flat season. Dave left everything in his hands and over the coming months Dave would name the filly and choose his racing colours etc. I had been down this road a few times and was able to tell him about all of the various procedures to be done prior the filly making a racecourse debut.

David and his wife Aine have two children at present, Jack and Caoimhe. He has been extremely successful in his career to-date and as a result was in a very good position to afford a racehorse. Everything in Dave's life had been working out to a tee but him and Aine were dealt with some bombshell news a few years ago when young Caoimhe was diagnosed with autism. Mind you, he was lucky to have such a good career, enabling him to give Caoimhe all of the professional care and attention required with an autistic child. Caoimhe is a lovely little girl and I'm glad to report that she is progressing very well at present. Not forgetting Jack of course, who is a really grand young fella and a mad Manchester United supporter just like his Uncle Skin. Dave, Aine and Jack have a pet name for Caoimhe at home, so she is affectionately known as *Miss Minnies*. So when it came to naming Dave's new horse it was a bit of a no-brainer and so the Fram filly who Dave, Jay and I had spent a few hours discussing and viewing on that fateful Saturday morning would become known as Miss Minnies and on hearing the name I thought to myself - Well, if there's a God in heaven and if my Da was looking down, then surely Miss Minnies deserved a stroke of luck, even if only for young Caoimhe's sake.

Miss Minnies was to thrive throughout the winter months and indeed the word from the trainer as soon as he started to work with her was encouraging to say the least. As the months progressed I visited the Curragh gallops on occasion with Dave and was able to watch both A Chuisle and Miss Minnies do their respective workouts having pre-arranged same with the two trainers. Miss Minnies was one of the those horses who would need some cut in the ground to be at her best so with the Irish summer ahead, Dave had a far better chance of his horse running before mine what with all the rain that we were having.

From July onwards, Miss Minnie was ready to run and was entered up to run her first race at, would you believe, the Galway races. My memories of Galway came flooding back on hearing the news of her entry so I told Dave that I hoped he had better luck than I had there with Penny and Me. Miss Minnies would run her first race in a two-year old auction maiden on the Friday evening of the Galway Racing Festival.

My nephew Paul's wedding was taking place on the same day so I wasn't able to attend. Dave travelled to Galway alone and would join the wedding party later that evening. The race would be shown live on Irish television and the full Kelly clan assembled in the hotel bar to see how she got on.

Miss Minnies had been working very well on the gallops and Dave was expecting a good introductory run based on the trainer's reports. We all had few bob each-way on her and she was well-fancied by the bookies to run into a place finish at odds of six-to-one or thereabouts. Dave had told me prior to the race that the plan was for her to go from the front from the very start in the seven-furlong event and indeed this was the case when the race commenced. Minnies took off at great speed and led the race right up to the last furlong. Because of the conditions of the race she was giving weight allowance to most of the other fancied horses in the race which included a few colts (male horses). Minnies ran very green which is normally the case with young two-year olds, particularly when they lead from the front with no other horse to accompany them. She was still right in it at the finish and it was only in the last two hundred yards that she became tired and was passed by three horses including the race favourite, leaving her to finish in fourth place, only a couple of lengths behind the winner. For her first race and having to do it the hard way from the front, this was a brilliant run from a two-year old filly and jockey Willie Supple, one of the best in the game, was more than pleased with her to say the least and gave very positive feedback to Dave on their return to the parade ring. He was of the opinion that it would only be a matter of time based on that run before Minnies would be visiting the winner's enclosure. Dave picked up one thousand euro for fourth place so all in all, it was tremendous start to his racing career as a first-time owner. I explained to him that he should realise how lucky he was as a lot of people including myself unfortunately have horses for years and never had any luck whatsoever with them. 'It's all about having a stroke of luck, Skin' was Dave's reply. I certainly didn't have any to-date so it was nice to see my youngest brother having a bit.

Miss Minnies came out of the race very well and ate up all of her food that night and after a few days rest she was back working on the gallops. David Myerscough picked out a few races for her and eventually decided on an auction maiden race for two year olds in Down Royal, just a few weeks after her first run, which was encouraging as she was fit and ready to go so soon afterwards.

Dave, Aine and Jack travelled to the races. I couldn't make it on the day, but made sure I was at home to watch on *At The Races* and having spoken in detail to Dave that morning it was obvious that a big run was expected from Minnies. There were just eight runners in the race and two in particular looked good on the form book and were short-priced first and second favourites as a result. Minnies was available at a price of six-to-one or thereabouts. I had a few bob on each-way and Dave had a fairly sizeable bet each-way also. At this price if she finished in the first three we were guaranteed our money back at least and judging from her Galway run I felt she should definitely be in the first three.

And they're off! Minnies of course is out like a bullet again and off she goes in front this time under young jockey Padraig Beggy. She looked comfortable in front and I was talking to the television again telling her and young Beggy not to go too fast and use up all her energy too early in the race. She was watching everything going on around her and turning into the home straight was still about a length in front. Time for all the jockeys to get serious and when they did the race was on in earnest. Minnies was still in front a furlong out but looked to be tiring a little as expected at which time one of the others loomed up beside her and passed her out. Padraig Beggy gave her a few little reminders with his whip and the other jockey was doing the very same with his so both young horses were being asked to giver their all. 'She's gonna be second' I thought as at this point she was still about half a length behind, but it was now a two-horse race. 'Come on Minnies' I shouted and all of a sudden under a hard drive, she started to fight back. Jesus, I couldn't believe how genuine she was and showed the heart of a lion to work her way back to the front just approaching the finish line and was still in front where it mattered with her ears pricked. Miss Minnies on just her second attempt was Dave's first winner. The stuff that dreams are made of in racehorse ownership. I was thrilled for him and her even though this was my dream also and after all the years I still hadn't accomplished the desired result. Here was the little filly owned by my youngest brother, called after his precious little daughter, initially viewed by Dave, Jay and I, out winning on an Irish racecourse on just her second attempt. Brilliant just brilliant! Minnies will run lots more times all going well and will step up in class along the way so hopefully before I finish there'll be more success to report!

Still Bloody Raining

I don't know what's gone wrong with Irish summers but the amount of rain currently falling is just unbelievable. The farmers are now in a state of panic as we are now into September and the harvest is still uncut in the fields and the ground is simply too wet to allow machinery to drive on. The news reports are headlined by floods and monsoon-like conditions making one wonder are we living in Ireland at all?

A Chuisle is costing me a small fortune to keep and all she is doing is her morning workout on the Curragh gallops and spending the rest of her time in the stable. All she needs is plenty of grub and if she had a television with all the channels she'd rightly be on the pig's back! We need to get her into a race very soon or else she will just have to be taken out of training and we can move on to plan B. The only problem being that we don't have a plan B. How do I get myself into these situations? If I take her out of training today, as sure as God, the sun will shine for the next month and the opportunity I was waiting for will pass me by. On the other hand if I do take her out at least it won't cost training fees at the end of the month. What does one do I ask myself! I'll give it to the end of the month and make my decision then. I'm not gonna worry about it in the interim. I almost believe that myself.

Time for Change

I am now out of work for the first time in twenty years. Ok, it was my own decision to take redundancy and yes I know I got a few bob as a result but my decision was made on the strength of commencing a new job which I was promised would be all in place in a matter of weeks after I left. I am now told that the weeks will more than likely now be months, so needless to say I am at a bit of a loose end. I was never one to sit around the house all day and have been keeping myself busy with all of the odd jobs that need doing.

I have to say that having spent sixteen years in the same job which I really enjoyed for at least the first fourteen of those years and decided to leave because of the changes such as outsourcing, which added a lot of stress to my job, that I am now looking at life from a completely different angle and realizing that life is far too short to spend most of it in the same office in the same four walls doing the same thing day in and day out. The new job I have in the pipeline (if it ever comes about) will allow me to arrange most of my appointments from home at times that will suit me and while I have every faith in doing the job to the very best of my ability in a type of customer service manager's role, it will allow me far more time once I have it up and running to spend more time doing the things I enjoy most. The one thing I do miss most though from my last job are all of the wonderful friends I made who became part of my life although I have every intention of keeping in contact and meeting up whenever possible.

So what are the things I enjoy most then?? Jay and Erica are just back from their three-month stint in Long Island in America, where they both worked in a restaurant for the summer. Jay is back to college this week and Erica is studying (well, supposed to be) for her solicitor's exams which she will sit next month. It's just Vera and I in the house most of the time and with me being there now all of the time while out of work and nothing but constant rain outside it can be interesting to say the least to keep smiling all of the time. Vera reckons that a few weeks away to somewhere nice, Prague being the latest idea is just what the doctor ordered while I am re-adjusting to life. Vera always reckons that a few weeks away to somewhere nice is a wonderful idea. I think had I married a bloody travel agent that I would not have travelled as much in my life. However this time and indeed most times I do agree that a bit of time away does help re-charge the batteries and get one motivated again. We as a family have travelled so much over the years that I certainly believe that it has broadened the minds of both Erica and Jay in particular and has given them a tremendous base on which to build their lives around. I know when I was their age I was lucky to get to the next town outside Athy but that's just the way it was back then. So the plan is a visit to Prague to re-charge the batteries and hope that when I get back that the rain will have stopped, allowing A Chuisle to get one more run to prove that she can do it and that my new job is in place, allowing me the opportunity to begin a whole new life as a result. Always the optimist eh!!

I will certainly get back to following the local football teams and who knows may even become involved in coaching again. I will definitely take off every Saturday from whatever job I go to as I have worked nearly every one of them in my last job. I am busy in the garden between the showers over the past few weeks and have every intention of spending most Saturday mornings in the fresh air, while pruning shrubs and hedges etc. and keeping the place looking its' best. I look forward to spending quality time with my other half and with Erica and Jay when they are home. The few pints at the week-end in the local bar are a must if only just to unwind and dare I say it I will spend as much time as I can enjoying horse-racing in some form or manner.

The flat-racing season in Ireland this year has been a disaster for owners, trainers and indeed the horse racing authority because of the consistent rain we've been having. This week alone has seen the cancellation of all meetings right up to Thursday. A couple of weeks ago the Curragh was abandoned which does not happen very often and last weekend's Champion Stakes meeting in Leopardstown, which is one of the biggest meetings on the racing calendar, was postponed on the Saturday and run on the Sunday instead. All of these changes and cancellations play havoc for the authorities with entries etc. so it has been a very frustrating time for all. In my case, as you know, I just cannot get a run for A Chuisle and probably the most frustrating part of it all is that she is currently in great form and 100% ready for a run. With all of the preparation work done it is soul-destroying for the trainer and owner as it can often be the case that some little thing can go wrong at any point and this is what all concerned are most afraid of coming up to any race fixture. Indeed just about six weeks ago the weather had improved enough to consider entering A Chuisle for a race but the day before entry she cracked a hoof in her morning workout on the Gallops, which set her back about three weeks. By the time the hoof was better we were lucky enough to get her entered and accepted for a maiden hurdle for mares only in Roscommon but wouldn't you know it, the heavens opened a couple of days before the race date and the meeting was abandoned as a result. Patience is a virtue!! The Curragh is scheduled for this week-end for the St. Leger meeting, with racing both Saturday and Sunday. This is not much use to me but I'm glad to report that Miss Minnies is entered up in two races, a two-year old handicap nursery and a two-year old listed event. Whichever she does run in will be a step up in class for her so more to follow on this next week.

When I first started up the racing syndicates, one of the main attractions for people to become involved was the fun aspect of the whole thing. Going to the races as an owner, seeing your own horse running, regardless of how he or she ran, having a joke and a laugh as a group and a few bets in each race on the card. With experience I have come to learn that unless you have all the luck in the world from day one, such as Dave had with Minnies, it can become more of an endurance test moreso than a bit of fun. If you do not have a horse who proves to be very good or at least good enough to finish in the business end of the race from its' very first outing, truth be told, you are probably better off with not having one at all. It is very important to potential owners to know this when they plan to start out and become involved. I think this is true right through to the whole breeding side of Irish racing. A lot of people in Ireland have had fillies/mares run for them on the track who proved that they were just not up to it. Of course I fall into this category and I hasten to add that there is no shame in owning such a horse. However, the problem is that a lot of these mares are then used for breeding and in most cases, regardless of which stallion one decides upon, the net result will be a similar type of horse, that more than likely will not make the grade either. Now I know there are exceptions to the rule and probably even a few of them whereby real good horses come from mediocre mares, but on the whole this is rare.

The outcome of breeding from such mares results in a lot of foals being brought to the sales and not even making enough to cover the cost of the stallion used, plus more being kept for racing. I have done this myself and learned the hard and expensive way. This is the main reason for so many I won't call them bad horses but rather so many horses who are quite simply are just not good enough. The sales are flooded with them. When they are kept for training the entries are flooded also, leading to far too many horses in the system who will never pay their way. This in turn means balloting, dare I mention the dreaded word and until the horse is rated out of the system the problem continues.

I know we all have to start somewhere but the point I'm making will save you a lot of money at the end of the day, if you take a realistic look at the mare you plan to breed from. If she was no good there is no point unless you have money to throw away. The question then becomes what do you do with such a mare?? This is the six marker question which has various suggested answers to, some which nobody wants to hear but at the end of the day she is better kept in the field as a pet if feasible to do so or else give her to somebody else who can keep her for free or whatever without breeding from her. I do emphasise that these are just my opinions on the subject of over-capacity in Irish racing/breeding and while I am no expert by any means, I am speaking from experience.

Just looking through the current entries for upcoming races gives an indication of how difficult it can be to get a run for an ordinary-type horse in Ireland. Dundalk's all-weather facility has been used to add extra fixtures to try compensate for those meetings which have been abandoned due to weather. A typical example is the entry list for the lowest grade handicap on one of the days. For horses rated 45 to 60, which as I say is the lowest grade on the flat in Ireland, there are eight-nine entries. Bear in mind that the maximum number of runners allowed for the race is somewhere around the fifteen-mark, so this will mean that from that list there will be over seventy horses who won't get into that race and will have to go through the same procedure again next time.

There is not a whole lot that H.R.I. can do as I have eluded to already, other than what they are doing at present and maybe some of the ideas I mentioned earlier might help, but one way or another this is a very serious problem in Irish racing at present, so let's hope it can improve going forward. One very important aspect of all of this also from an owner's perspective is that it cost the very same amount to keep a bad horse in training as it does to keep a good one. I can guarantee you that from that list of eighty-nine there are plenty of horses who are crying out for a run, or should I say their owners and trainers are and who by the time they do get into a race, will have some little thing go wrong, preventing them from taking part.

However, enough doom and gloom for the moment. This is still a wonderful sport and Ireland is still the number one ambassador in thoroughbred racing worldwide. The exploits this year alone of Aidan O'Brien, Johnny Murtagh and the Coolmore/Ballydoyle team are almost unbelievable. They have already won something like seventeen group one races around the world. Jim Bolger's team have also picked up their share of group winners, including the Epsom Derby and Irish Champion Stakes with their horse called *New Approach.* I won't even try mention the names of all of Aidan O'Brien's winners. In Cheltenham last March, there were Irish winners and the winner of the Gold Cup, while trained in the UK, was indeed Irish-bred. I realise I am referring to the very top races in the world, but at the end of the day, while any owner will settle for any type of a winner, (well within reason), one involved with horse racing can never aim too high with their dreams. We know they may never come through but without them, life becomes too predictable and sometimes boring.

The sun is shining outside my window at present. I repeat, the sun is shining outside at present. I've just had a cup of tea and as I sat enjoying it, the weather forecast came on the telly. Sunshine in all areas this afternoon will continue into the evening and tomorrow morning HOWEVER tomorrow afternoon will see the return of showers (some heavy at times) and the outlook for Sunday is for a continuation of unsettled patterns. Holy divine Jesus, I think I'll move to Turkey or somewhere before I go mad. Of course, apart from not liking the rain for all the obvious reasons, my primary frustration is because I cannot get a race for the horse. In my frustrated state, I ring Valerie and lay it on the line that this weather is dragging on far too long and I'm afraid I have no option but to take A Chuisle out of training. Valerie agrees and says 'I don't blame you, it is just not worth the hassle'. Unless some miracle happens between now and end of this month, A Chuisle will never run again, well not under my name anyway. Another one bites the dust!! No fairytale ending again and still no winner. Well at least Miss Minnies is the first winner in the family and I will be following her progress with great enthusiasm starting this week-end.

The tips are still coming in fast and furious by the way! This week alone I have received information on six horses who are supposed to win. Unfortunately the horses are not as fast and furious as the information is. Not a single one of them have won and luckily enough I kept my money in my pocket this time. The sixth one ran just a few minutes ago in Tramore so I decided to watch the race as I was watching television at the time. Having studied the race earlier in the day on receipt of the tip, I quite fancied the horse in question. I was very tempted to have a bet, but decided to let the horse run without the extra weight of my money on. Even on the television it was very obvious that the racing ground was very soft as the sods were being thrown up left, right and centre throughout the race. The tip took up the running in the last furlong and I was cursing myself at this point for not having a bet as the horse was a decent price at odds of around five to one. However in the last fifty yards or so one sprouted wings from the rear and somehow or another got up to win by a nose. There's always one, I thought to myself (a saying quite often used in the gambling game) and at the same time while I was hoping he would win for the friend who gave me the tip, I was quite pleased with my own decision not to bet. Naturally enough, the phone rang immediately from my friend (my very irate friend at this point):

'Were you watching the race? Well, fuck it anyway, I thought he had it. Did you have a few bob on yourself?'

'Course I did' said I.

When someone gives you the odd good tip, never tell them you didn't back or you'll never get another one. Mind you, I'm not sure whether or not I'm right in saying that. A lot of the time you'd be far better off never hearing another horse's name from them again.

The thing about horseracing, as in most other sports, is that it brings people together and long-term friendships are formed from those with the same interests. In racing though, I find it intriguing, maybe just because there are so many types of races in so many different countries, with so many runners in each race, by so many different sires/dams and with varying ground conditions etc. that to sit down, study form, or indeed just pick one that you think will win and then to watch it winning is a very special feeling. Especially if it's a very good price. As a good friend of mine says:

'There's nothing sweeter than a good winner'.

Then there's the reading up on and gathering of information, be it for betting or just for interest or indeed for becoming involved in ownership or whatever. I have often spent hours surfing the internet or studying sales catalogues and sales results or reading the Racing Post or Irish Field, just compiling information to keep in my head on the wonderful world of thoroughbred horses. I've spent hours also with friends discussing such a winner or such a race or who the top stallion of different age groups of horses is. Actually in my phone address book, when I see who's calling, I can tell first of all from the name that it's about horses and depending on who it is I can tell whether it's a tip or whether it's information on a certain sire and so on.

One of the lads only ever rings with tips. In all the years I have known him he has never once spoken to me about anything else other than word he has on some horse that's a good thing. There are times he would drive you mad. He has often given me ten tips in a row who were nowhere and when he eventually hits on a winner he'd ask:

'Where would you be without me?'

The funny thing is he rings all of the other lads as well, not just me, with the same tips. He's a gas man and would back two flies going up a window and more than likely would have a tip for the second!

Another friend has the strangest bets and how he thinks of them is beyond me. I mean this guys betting slip always contains at least six and sometimes maybe as many as ten horses. Most people who back horses would be familiar with doubles, trebles, Yankees, patents, cross-doubles and trebles etc. but this fella will have the likes of 25 x 20 cent trebles, 5 x €1 four-horse accumulator and maybe some five-horse accumulators plus one single accumulator not to mention the doubles and trebles and God knows what included. I often told him over the years that if his bet ever comes up he'll have his name over the door of the shop. In recent weeks however he as clicked a few times and indeed took a fair few thousand euros from the bookies. How the girls working in the office are able to calculate his winnings, I will never understand. Fair play to him, though, he's won a lot more on the horses this year than anybody I know of. I told him there is no point explaining his bets to me because when I see them written down even I still can't understand them.

Next up are a few of the lads who watch horses for weeks on end and wait until what they calculate will be the horse's big day out. Time for a plunge, they say. They will have the form worked out to a tee and

Jason rides out the finish on his treasured hobby horse in full racing attire.

"Lester Piggott "My Hero" on the way to the weight room
after bringing home another winner.

Chatting with Hector in Eyre Square, Galway
on the Sunday prior to Penny and Me's Run at the Galway Races.

Badly hungover and having been soaked in the rain I'm given a hug from the one
and only Johnny Murtagh much to the amusement of Jason (left)
and trainer Michael Halford (right).

Jason leads in a mare and foal at Fortbarrington Stud.

A young Jason with one of the foals.

Jason shows our precious Soviet Star foal at Goffs Sales.

Where it all began: Curtsey and her first foal by Soviet Star.

Marc and Jason check the mares and foals in the paddocks.

Erica and Jason at the races in Nad al Sheba track in Dubai.

Mam and Dad pictured at their 50th Wedding Anniversary Party.

My beloved Dad studys the form stands at Gowran Park Races. Little did I know that this would be his last race meeting. God Rest Him !

*David, Jack and Aine pictured with **Miss Minnies***
*in the winners enclosure following her win in **Down Royal**.*
Also in the picture is Padraig Beggy (Jockey) and Minnies' stable assistant Ciara.

Penny and n   ft) and A Chuisle Mo Chroí
on their way bac   morning work on the Curragh.

Horses on the Curragh.

*Left to Right: Paul, Siobhán, Stephanie, Vera and myself
in Galway Parade Ring.*

the money ready when all the boxes are ticked. Not a word to anyone but the select few. Hundreds of euros on morning prices, on first shows with greater returns paid in specific offices. Spend the whole day going from shop to shop viewing prices, looking for the best odds. Military precision before the money is down. The horse never wins for them! They spend the next few weeks watching some horse that finished second before and the whole project swings into action again. The bookie loves to see them coming.

Last of all there's the professional, well he thinks he is anyway. He was telling me the other day that he has backed every one of O'Brien's group-one winners this year. He never mentions the fact that he has backed every one of O'Brien's runners this year. Work it out yourself!! He loves the big races, such as the classics, and if he backs the winner of one of them he never shuts up about if for the week.

'I told you all that such a horse would win' he'd say.

He's harmless really, but he gets on peoples' nerves by times, especially when they are losing. There may be one or two exceptions to the rule as in most things in life, but I think it's a true saying that you will never make money backing horses! I worked for a few years with a man named Joe Conlan, God be good to him, as he passed away a few years ago. Joe was renowned for not believing in throwing away money on backing horses and used always say to me:

'I guarantee you one thing, Skin, if there are a few rusty bikes outside the bookie office and a brand new Merc parked in front of them, when the bookie walks out, you won't see the bollox getting up on one of the bikes!'

Just about sums it up alright, Joe. He's probably looking down on us all and still laughing.

A wet Sunday
in the Curragh

Miss Minnies, fresh from her first win in only her second race had her next race in the Curragh on a very wet Sunday afternoon. Being a winner, it was easy to get her into a race and indeed she was entered for two races on this day so it was up to the trainer and David to decide which one she would contest. The short-term objective for her was to get one more run into her in Ireland before bringing her to Ascot in the UK for a two-year old sales race for all yearlings bought in the UK the previous year. Minnies had come from the Doncaster sales originally and so was eligible for entry in this race. David had her entered and all the entry fees paid so we were looking forward to a trip to Ascot. First of all, though, was the matter at hand of the Curragh run. She was entered in a listed race and in a nursery handicap. The listed race would have been a sizeable step up in grade but as I said to David it was tremendous start to even consider her for this event. To win or be placed in the first three in a listed event would mean having some black type added to her pedigree, making her a lot more valuable and a sound breeding prospect for future years. David and the trainer however decided to go for the nursery just to give her a chance with a more gradual approach, while all the time focussing on the end-goal of the Ascot run. The Ascot race, by the way, had a huge prize fund of £250,000 (sterling) with valuable prize money paid to the first ten finishers.

The weather for today's race was deplorable to say the least, as it had been for the two weeks previous, so the ground was extremely soft to heavy and it was actually touch and go as to whether Minnies would run at all. Eventually the lads decided to let her take her chance. Nine or ten of us including my Mam travelled over for the day but the rain meant we were confined to the restaurant area as it was uncomfortable to say the least to even try get to the parade ring or even to watch the races from the stands. Minnies would run in the fifth race on the card but the confidence levels were low due to the heavy conditions on the track, made even worse by the fact that four other races had already taken place. We all had a few quid each-way on her but only as an interest bet. She had a fairly wide draw and there were twenty-odd runners in the race, so all in all it was a big ask for her to be as competitive as she had already proven. When the race started Minnies was well out the back from the very start and it was obvious to me at this early stage that she wasn't enjoying herself. She had run her two previous races from the front and on much better ground. As the race progressed she made no impression at all and indeed Chris Hayes, the jockey, was very easy on her for the whole of the race. She finished around nineteenth and first impressions were that she just didn't handle the ground and hopefully there would be no other reason. Mind you, the horse that won the race had actually finished fourth in the race that Minnies won, so I thought maybe there is some little thing amiss with her.

Minnies ate up the night after the race and was examined by the vet early the following week. The fact that she was eating properly was a good sign so hopefully it was the ground after all. The plan for Ascot two weeks later was still in place and nearing the time David, Jay and I were arranging flight times to Heathrow etc. Jay was very excited as we all were I suppose to be visiting Ascot for the first time and the fact that we were associated with a runner made it all the more exciting. We were looking up the entries to see what horses were in the race, seeing what the weather forecast was in the UK and making sure that the ground wouldn't be like that in the Curragh. Jay had received permission from the college for the day off. I was still out of work so I could travel and David had arranged the day off from his job. David rang me on the Tuesday and I was expecting to find out flight times and the itinerary for the day, so I was excited to see his name on the caller ID.

'Well, Dave, what's the story? Are we all set for Friday?'

'Sorry, Skin, change of plan'.

'Oh, I don't like the sound of this'.

David then explained that the report from the vets blood test had shown that Minnies was carrying some sort of an infection and unfortunately this would rule her out for the big day on Friday. I was so disappointed as I was looking forward to it so much, but at the same time it was good to know that there was a reason for her poor run in the Curragh and at least it was better to know before her big day rather than find out after the race and maybe after another poor showing. I rang Jason straight away and after a few curses we said 'Ah, we'll have another day to come'.

Horses! Never straightforward.

One good thing that did happen around this time was the the rain had stopped and at long last we were having a bit of proper summer. Two full weeks of dry weather with a nice bit of sunshine thrown in for good measure. I should have known this would happen as soon as I decided to take A Chuisle out of training. The fact that we now had good ground available however now meant that we could have a look at the fixture list to see if there was a suitable race just to give her a second run over hurdles even if only for peace of mind. We entered her for a race in Navan and for one in Clonmel the following day. She was fit enough and in good form and had not run now for four months. Luckily enough she got into the Navan race, which was a two-and-half mile hurdle race for mares only, from 4 year olds and upwards. At this stage we had decided that this would be her last race unless she surprised us all by finishing in the first three. There were thirty runners in the race and she was the youngest horse in the race so to be honest, I didn't give her much of a chance in what was a very decent race. None of us went to the race, so we watched it on television on a Saturday afternoon. To see the thirty runners line up at the start gave me a true indication of the size of the task facing a young four-year old filly in only her second run over timber. Nicky O'Shea was our jockey and on discussion with him it was decided to keep her fairly well up with the pace and on the outside if possible to avoid any danger. Nicky worked this to a tee and A Chuisle ran up with the first group of about sixteen horses and he steered her around the outside for the whole of the race. She jumped really well from the start and it was obvious to me that this indeed was her game and in hindsight we probably should not have bothered running her on the flat at all and should have just let her grow and commence her national hunt campaign when she reached her current age of four. Hindsight is a great thing and I hasten to add that it was nobody's fault that we chose the route we did. A Chuisle finished in twelfth position having jumped perfect and was staying on really well at the finish. Twelfth of thirty in only her second hurdle race was quite a decent run and Nicky was very pleased with her and was adamant that she needed an even longer distance to be at her best, as he said he had a difficult job pulling her up after the race. 'Now where does that leave us', I thought to myself, bearing in mind that we had agreed beforehand that unless she finished in the first three that was that. Jason and my brother-in-law Marc were quick to point out that she should have been hurdling only and that she may be good enough to pick up a handicap hurdle at least. My friend Pat Abbey texted me to say on the evidence of that run she was definitely worth another try. Nicky O'Shea said he had sat on horses much worse than her and that she may be worth continuing with, so all in all I didn't know what to think. Valerie was very pleased with the run, genuinely, and said, at the end of the day, the decision was mine. I decided to play it by ear for a couple of days and would make my decision then. I thought as did Marc and Jay that if we could get her straight back into a race within a week or two that she would definitely improve no end with the benefit of the run under belt.

The following Monday morning I awoke to the sound of rain falling on the roof of the house and looking outside was greeted by a miserable wet morning. 'That's all I fuckin' need' I thought to myself.

After breakfast I decided to have a quick look at the upcoming fixtures list on the laptop and indeed had a look at the long-term weather forecast. Bad news looked back at me on both accounts. There was to be no suitable race for A Chuisle for at least a month and the weather forecast was brutal. Rain between the showers type of thing. My mind was made up at long last. The news headlines around now were full of despair. The American economy was in turmoil, with talks of billion-dollar bailouts from government for financial institutions. This was having a spiral effect right around the world and Ireland needless to say was no exception. The talk here was of job losses, company closures, slowdowns in the thriving building economy and indeed on this very day it was made official that Ireland was now in a recession. Recession, generally referred to as the 'R' word, had not been spoken of since the early eighties here and we as a nation had just enjoyed the Celtic Tiger era, during which we became one of the fastest-growing countries in the world. Times were changing, the future was bleak and people were being advised to tighten their belts. I was now out of work, admittedly by my own choice, but with nothing but bad news all round on the jobs front the last thing I needed was to be dipping into my few bob redundancy money to keep a horse in training. Especially a horse who wouldn't be running, particularly now that the autumn/winter season was now upon us. I found myself becoming a bit depressed and in bad form (not my style), between rain and horses and recessions and job losses and being out of work myself, so it was time to face reality. I rang Valerie later that day and this time it was the end of the road for A Chuisle. I explained the fixtures/weather situation and in fairness she saw my point completely. I wasn't sure what I would do with the horse and I have to say that all the time in the back of my mind somewhere I had visions of some other fucker taking up the reins from where I left off and having lots of success with her after I had done all the donkey work. However, the decision was made – A Chuisle my chroi, whom I had bred from a baby, would not be my first winner either, unfortunately. I could have brought her home to Fortbarrington, but for the moment she would go to pasture on Valerie's land and hopefully we would find somebody interested in her rather than having to go the sales route again, with what was a mediocre horse at the end of the day. Will I ever get sense??? Would you believe that in the last few days just after deciding to take the horse out of training, first of all I met an old friend who grew up just down the road from me and who now happens to work full-time in horseracing as a trainer's assistant and she asked me if I was interested in becoming involved in a racing syndicate. Secondly, another friend from my own syndicate also rang to say he had bought a share in a very well-bred four-year old national hunt horse and that they needed one more member for the syndicate and would that be me? I said to both of them that if they wanted to have any luck with their horses that they should leave me out of it as the only luck I've had with horses has been bad luck.

I decided to take a large step back from racehorse ownership, at least for the present, to give myself a chance to catch my breath and to start enjoying racing again for a change and not be worrying over meeting trainer bills, H.R.I. statements, watching bad weather forecasts and scrolling through fixture lists. The yearling sales are currently taking place in Goffs so I decided to call there and view the future champions at their infancy stage. I have always been intrigued with the sales of yearlings in particular. I was told in no uncertain circumstances, by the way, to keep my two hands in my pockets at the sales. From day one I watched the big players in the game to see which bloodlines they wanted, some of which sell for vast amounts of money. One sold yesterday for instance, for €500,000 and I love taking the details of these horses, just to follow their progress as they grow up and begin racing. Not just the expensive or should I say the really expensive ones, but also ones that I like and would like to be able to buy for reasonable money, just to see would I have picked the right ones. This has always been a hobby of mine and Jason is even more interested than I am. I suppose this is why I took the plunge all those years ago and bought the mare in foal, in the hope of great things to come. Having been there, albeit on a smallish scale in comparison to the big guns, it has made me even more interested in following the various bloodlines. Maybe someday I'll be lucky enough to be in a position to strike gold in some form or manner with the horses. With my notes in hand, I leave the sales and the most important thing is that I've had a very enjoyable day out. On returning home, the first thing I hear is:

'Don't tell me you bought a horse!'

Stern words, I better stay away from ownership for a while at least.

What now, Skinner?

What now is right. As I alluded to earlier, the country is now in recession and I'm thinking it ironic that the timing of having to take the horse out of training, having left my job, all happening at the same time, is just my luck at the moment. When I decided to leave my job I left with the promise of a very good job in a matter of weeks from a friend of mine, who I had dealt with over the years. Unfortunately, the downturn in the economy resulted in this job not being as readily available as promised. So there I am, sitting at home everyday, wondering just what the future holds. I now have a four-year old filly whom I can't exactly move into the spare room and who is costing money to keep even out of training. Miss Minnies is also finished for the season and will not resume her racing career until next March. Not only have I lost my daily routine of going to work, but I have also lost the time and interest of following the horses progress, which was my main hobby for the past few years. Now I am well aware that there are lots of people with far bigger problems in their lives than I have at present, but still I have now reached that wall which I haven't seen for many a year.

Watching television the other night, I saw and an advertisement for GAA football and the narrator read the Rudyard Kipling poem '*If*' and these particular lines held specific resonance to my life at present.

'If you can dream and not make dreams your master,

If you can think and not make thoughts your aim.

If you can meet with triumph and disaster

And treat those two imposters just the same!'

Just for one split-second it was as though these words were being whispered into my ear from my Dad above and lodged in my brain, in a way which made me feel positive, feel like my old self and once again become the eternal optimist which I have always been, for better or worse. I thought it's not the end of the world, far from it. There's no shame in losing once. I've tried my best and the dreams were still there, which would make the taste of victory all the sweeter, should it come my way.

So onwards and upwards and first things first. My first and primary objective is to get back to work and while I still might take up the job I was offered when it eventually becomes available, I have decided not to leave all of my eggs in one basket, by looking for work at every available opportunity. Having been in my last job for sixteen years, I had lost touch with the whole job recruitment side of things and indeed had not updated my curriculum vitae in all of that time. I was advised to keep my CV short, precise and to the point. On hearing this advice, I remember thinking of my best man's speech at my brother David's wedding when I used the lines:

'A good speech (or in this case a good CV),

Should be like a good woman's mini-skirt,

That is, it should be long enough to cover the essentials,

And short enough to keep everybody interested'.

It's not very easy to cover the essentials of a sixteen-year career and keep it short and interesting for the person reading it. However, after lots of thought and effort along with the assistance of the two women in my life, both wife and daughter, I finally ended up with a presentable two pages, which covered my working career, without it being too long to cover everything.

With CV now in hand, it allowed me to begin applying for jobs of all descriptions. I felt I was being pro-active and not just waiting for the jobs to come looking for me. All I need now is to be successful with at least one of the applications. Thereafter my plan of action will be to get myself back to a financially secure position and while making sure that all of the priorities such as Jay's education, Erica's start in the real world, not forgetting the day-to-day bills and upkeep of the house and cars are looked after, to mention but a few, somewhere deep down in my plans will be to start from scratch with horse number whatever it is at this stage, so fingers crossed. I'm not sure how this will be received at home, so here's hoping it's a really good job that comes along.

The current crop of foals in Fortbarrington are almost ready to be sold in the Goffs November foal sales. There is quite a lot of preparatory work with the foals in order to have them looking their best and behaving properly on the day of the sales. I am helping out with them at the moment and this mainly involves teaching them how to walk properly on a lead rope. This is all completely new to such young horses and it can be hard work as they can be quite nervous at first and even though they are only babies, they are still strong enough to make life difficult for the person handling them. Jason has spent the last few years working with the mares and foals and as soon as he comes home from college each week-end, it is straight out to the yard with Marc to discuss the progress of each one. Indeed, this year, Marc and Jay travelled to Kentucky sales for the first time, where Marc bought two really nice well-bred mares in foal to top stallions. The resulting two colt foals are included in those now being prepared for sale. Two gorgeous foals I hasten to add, and Jay is adamant that one in particular is worth an awful lot of money. I must say he really does stand out and is more like a two-year old at this stage. I was at my very best to control him and while he was walking perfectly I was almost running such is his strength. Each time I lead him for maybe thirty minutes fast-pace walking, I am almost out of breath by the time I put him back in the stables. The foals are out in the paddocks for most of the day so by the time we walk them each evening, all they want to do is get back to the stable, where they know at this stage that their food is waiting for them. Knowing that they are about to be fed makes them very excited and you need to be in the full of your health to show them who's in charge while walking them.

It's amazing how different each foal is and they all have their own individual personalities. The oldest foal in this crop, at least a month or two even older than the others, just so happens to be the smallest of the group. He is actually a lot smaller that the others. Because of this he is probably the least valuable, although it is hard to know at this point. He is very well-bred, so he might surprise every one of us when it comes to the sales day. This little fellow happens to be my favourite however, not just because he is small, but he must be the friendliest and best-mannered foal I have ever seen. It is so easy to do any work with him as I can walk straight up to him without any fuss, get him ready for walking or to bring in from the paddock and when he walks he is more like a pet lamb than a young thoroughbred. Mind you, he is still all horse and for his size is amazingly strong. If he doesn't make his reserve price at the sales he would be the very type I would be interested in procuring for myself. Have to get the new job first, however, and time is running out.

G.A.A. Sunday

Last Sunday week was a very big day for my local GAA club. As I mentioned earlier, I spent almost ten years coaching underage football for my home team Athy. During this time, we had tremendous success at under-ten, twelve, fourteen, but beyond that age group the competition became unbelievably strong and as a result it was very difficult to win tournaments without having top-of-the-range facilities and indeed top-of- the-range players. Not unlike horseracing, I suppose. I had brought under-sixteen teams to finals and minor (under-18) teams to semi-finals, but was never lucky enough to win the prize, having come so close on a few occasions. Many coaches before me had suffered the same consequences, but as is the case with Gaelic football, it is a huge part of Irish culture in every county, so we never gave up.

This Sunday was the first time in a good few years that our minor team had reached the final and the excitement around the town was at fever-pitch, such is the following of the game. Many businesses and houses were proudly decorated in the red-and-white colours of Athy and these young sixteen to eighteen year-olds were the pride of the town, having reached the final. To go and win the championship final at minor level would be a major boost for the club but we were underdogs to do so against a Newbridge team who had looked awesome in their semi-final victory. We had lost many finals to Newbridge teams down the years, so the scent of victory would be all the sweeter should it come about today. There has always been a great friendly rivalry between Newbridge teams Sarsfields and Moorefield with Athy. Having worked in Newbridge myself for so long, I can tell you that the slagging and banter over the years with work-mates and friends has always been intense and this at the end of the day is what GAA football is all about and why it will always be so popular here.

This Sunday's final was against Sarsfields and prior to the match I had a few calls and texts from my Newbridge fans telling me that they thought this year's minor team were exceptional and would be very difficult to beat. Sarsfields had won the minor championship last year, so would enter the fray as champions. A lot of the Athy team today had played under my management over the latter stages of my involvement and to be honest I knew deep down, having watched these lads progress, that we were not just going to the County Grounds in Newbridge to make up the numbers. Amazingly, it has been thirty-five years since we won a minor championship in Athy, which says two things. First of all, how difficult it is to win and secondly how hungry we were for it. Could this be our year?? I had kept very quiet about my opinions as I was now just a spectator with no direct involvement and Jay was now over-age and playing Under-21 and senior football, so all in all I hadn't seen too much of the games leading up to the final. However, I had seen enough to form my own opinion, which was that the Newbridge lads were in for the game of their lives to prevent our lads lifting the cup at the end of this one. Over the years, Athy G.A.A. has had many stalwarts and indeed many loyal supporters, who literally ate and drank both Athy club and Kildare county football. My late Dad was one of these people and unfortunately there were quite a few others, some very recently who had also passed away. Such was the passion for this game that many of these names were mentioned and thought fondly of prior to the big day. Athy have not won a senior championship since 1989 and when I was involved with management it was always widely thought that the only way we were ever going to get back to the good times was to start from scratch with the very young players at our disposal. All of our team today have been playing since under-eight and ten years, so it is rather pleasing to see the fruits of many volunteers labours come to fruition. These young fellas have enjoyed success at almost all levels except for todays level, so I was certainly of the opinion that win, lose or draw, each and every one of them would play from the heart.

The game was to start at 1.30pm and would be followed by the senior final at 3pm. There was a tailback of traffic in Athy from 12.30pm onwards for the short 19-mile trip to the county grounds in Newbridge. A sea of red-and-white flags graced the main Dublin road heading out of the town. It was a very wet and windy afternoon and I wasn't sure whether or not these conditions would suit us. I thought for a minute 'Don't tell me the heavy, wet ground is going to deprive me of victory at the football the same as it always did with the horses!' However, there was no room today for negative thoughts, so I let the adrenalin build up with confidence. I remember it took what seemed like an age to find a fuckin' space in Newbridge, so I knew that the home support would be huge for Sarsfields. This didn't bother me much, however, as we had our own army of support today. It did bother me though that I drove around for nearly twenty minutes looking for a fuckin' parking space. Eventually I found one and by the time I got into the stands, there were no seats left, so we stood for the game. I was surrounded by lots of Athy people mixed with a good few Sarsfields supporters so the banter was lively. Indeed on my way in I had a few shouts from my Newbridge colleagues from various sections of the stands all wishing me commiserations prior to a ball being even kicked. I spotted my brother Gerry among a large section of supporters and he gave me a wave and a clenched fist as much as to say 'This is our day!' I gave him one back, at which a Sarsfields fan and friend of mine shouted:

'You better do all your celebrating before the match, Skin!'

By Jesus, by the time I got to my position, the hair on the back of my neck was Bob Marley style. 'Come on, Athy' I shouted as our lads took to the pitch. 'Show these lads what you're made of'. A few Sarsfields fans shouted back at me in a sporting, but tense manner:

'You won't be shouting for long. Come on, the *Sash*' as they are known as. The rivalry had begun on the terraces and seconds later the ball was thrown in. Both sets of supporters shouting for their teams simultaneously made for an exciting hour to come.

Our lads had won the toss and decided to play with the wind in their backs for the first half. It was crucial that we got lots of scores with the wind as the pressure would be on us for the second half, playing against it. I thought that unless we were well in front at half-time, we well may be in trouble. It was obvious right from the start that our lads were really up for it today, as they fought for possession as though their lives depended on it. However it was also obvious to me that the opposition had some real quality players. As a result, as is always the case with me, I was a bundle of nerves and shouted at the top of my voice particularly at some of the referee's decisions. The ref was right most of the time as it turns out, but in the heat of the moment, every time he gave a decision against us, I called him all sorts.

Athy started so well that I was fearing the worst, in the sense that we were playing our trump cards too soon. There was no way, in my mind, that our lads could stay playing the type of excellent football they were playing, for the full game. I won't mention names as this was a team effort, but with excellent points coming from every angle, even the Sarsfields fans could be heard whispering:

'Jaysus, lads, these boys are good, we could be in trouble here'.

'Come on, Athy' I shouted till I became hoarse.

Some young girls close by were singing: 'Come on the Reds' and I thought for a moment of how disappointing it would be to lose after such a tremendous start. The referee blew his whistle for half-time and the scoreboard read:

ATHY: 9 Points   SARSFIELDS: 2 Points

I was dreading the thoughts of the second half, all the time thinking of the wind assistance.

During the half-time break there was lots of chat among both sets of supporters and the guy commentating for the local radio was of the opinion that this game was far from over and expected a big comeback from Sarsfields in the second half.

'Great minds think alike' I thought.

Ten minutes or so later and both teams returned for thirty minutes that would decide the champions of 2008. Thirty-five years we've been waiting for this and now it's only half an hour away, if the lads just stay focussed and do the simple things correctly. The tension among the Athy supporters was so tense that one would swear we were a mile behind. Truth of the matter was we were a mile ahead, but terrified of letting it slip now.

The second half began and straight away Sarsfields were on top of their game and realized that they needed to go up a gear if they were to turn things around at this point. They scored two points to narrow the gap to five, but I was still confident that we could hold out. A long kick in looked very dangerous and I was sure there was a goal on the cards for Sarsfields but our goalkeeper made a terrific catch and his excellent distribution set us on the counter-attack. Fast, brisk and accurate passing caught the eye of any admiring football fan and the last pass was so precise that it left our half-forward on his own with just the keeper to beat. I thought maybe just tap it over the bar for a sure point but he carried the ball at pace and at the last second the ball skipped away from him and just as I let out a curse, he cheekily stretched and fisted the ball over the keeper's head and to the back of the net for a smashing goal. 1 goal and 9 points to 4 points with eighteen minutes left. No way are we leaving this one behind. Sarsfields to their credit threw everything at our lads and scored a few more but a second goal followed by a few points in succession left the final score at 2-11 to 0-9 and at long last the long wait was finally over. Grown men had a tear in their eye and hundreds of jubilant supporters ran through the gates and onto the pitch, including myself, to congratulate the lads on a splendid exhibition of Gaelic football. Each and everyone of the players cried with delight, such was the relief of their long, hard efforts, to eventually bring back a minor championship title to Athy. Bill Shankly, a famous Liverpool manager once said that

'Football is not a matter of life and death, it is far more important than that'. We were so hungry to win today that it was easy to understand exactly what he meant. I have to say that all of my Sarsfields friends and/or workmates were quick to ring me on the mobile to congratulate us or what they also described as an exhibition of football played as it should be. Our captain finally got his hands on the coveted cup and made a terrific speech, which just about summed up what this meant to every Athy G.A.A. supporter. We headed back to the town later, where celebrations began in earnest and over lots of pints and laughs, the overriding feeling was that hopefully this is just the beginning of things to come. What a day!! Well done, lads!!

I must admit that the sweet taste of success gave me a great lift and I remember thinking that this would be very similar to eventually owning the elusive winner in my horseracing exploits. I also remember thinking that at this point I've been involved with horses for almost seven years, so I only have another twenty-eight years to wait!!!

Oh Lord, will I ever get sense??

Prague

For the long week-end in October, my wife and I decided to head off to the Czech Republic for the few days. My wife as you know has the travel bug and for me it was an opportunity to recharge the batteries so to speak. We decided on Prague as we hadn't been there before and Erica had visited it not so long ago and thought we would really enjoy it. I knew nothing of the place or the country as such so I couldn't wait to arrive. It was just over a two-hour flight from Dublin and our flight was at 7.15am on the Thursday morning, which meant I had to wake at 4.30ish am to be at Dublin airport in time. Having a shower and shave at 4 in the morning is not exactly my cup of tea, but as with all trips away, the adrenalin kicks in to keep one going.

On arrival in Prague, I knew straight away that I was really going to enjoy these few days. Our hotel, called 'The Riverside' was excellent in every aspect and the location was just perfect. The tram system in the city was very convenient and very good value, so it was great to have the option of either a nice short walk along the river to many of the sights to behold such as the castle, the Charles bridge, or we could hop on the tram and be there and see lots of other architectural sights within a matter of minutes. Prague was crowded with tourists from all over the globe and with the lovely, fine, dry, brisk touch of perfect Autumn weather, all in all it was a type of medieval fairytale to enjoy, which we really did.

The only downside of my visit to Prague was that it coincided with the running of the annual Breeders' Cup classic races in America, for which many of the top European flat horses travel over for. Having followed the season so carefully, both Jay and I keenly awaited this event. To be perfectly honest, when we decided on the week-end away, I totally forgot that it clashed with the Breeders' Cup and for my personal safety I felt it best not to mention this at home, what with all of the trouble I had gotten myself into over the years with these horses. Jay watched the races live or ATR and because of the time difference, they were shown very late at night. However, I did arrange with Jay that via text he would keep me up to date with the various results. In the main event of the evening, Jay and the lads from Fortbarrington had a huge interest, as their best foal in the yard, whom I referred to earlier (the one more like a two-year old) is a son of the same stallion named *Elusive Quality* as the English horse in the race called *Raven's Pass*. Victory for Raven's Pass in this international group-one event would help enormously in the interest and indeed value of such a smashing foal from the same stallion. This was also the foal, or should I say one of the foals which Marc and Jay had travelled to Kentucky for last autumn, where they brought home the in-foal mares. Mind you, next week they are off to Kentucky again for the 2008 sale. Jay had a small bet on Raven's Pass and I actually forgot to back him before I left. He was at very good odds to win but the competition was of the highest quality, including last year's winner and also the multiple group-one winning Irish horse from the all-conquering Aidan O'Brien yard called *Henry the Navigator*, who had beaten Raven's Pass before, but on their last duel, Raven's Pass had actually come out on top. Because of all the form to-date plus the foal which Jay has always thought to be a future superstar, this was an intriguing race. Unfortunately in Prague there was no TV coverage, so being one hour ahead also there meant I was tucked up in bed at the time of the race. I was awoken around 12:30am by the beeping of my phone on receipt of a text. The text simply read: "Raven's Pass won. Told you he was a good thing 8/1". I replied: 'You're some man to pick horses. Good Night'. As I went back to sleep I was thrilled for Jay, apart from his bet, his heart and soul is in the Elusive Quality foal and he was instrumental with Marc in the purchase of the mare in Kentucky last year. I know one swallow never made a summer and the same applies in racing as in one winner never made a stallion but with such an exceptional foal, the vibes just couldn't be better, so if anything it will be interesting to see the final outcome. Will let you know soon enough.

Speaking of International Group One winners etc. is all very well and indeed is what top flat-racing is all about and why after all I am so interested in the whole thing. Meanwhile however, I'm right down at the bottom of the scale and as of today I have no takers for A Chuisle so I have no alternative but to enter her in the sales in December. In the interim she is costing me money to keep so I'm hoping that she at least sells at the sales and hopefully I get enough to cover all current bills. Again I have no intention of putting people or syndicates etc. off becoming involved in racehorse ownership but hopefully my experience to-date may help even one potential owner be fully aware of all of the pros and cons of having your own horse. I have learned the hard way as you know over the years but having said all that it's still in my blood somehow so I'll probably never give up. Regardless of your knowledge in horses there is one thing you need to have to be successful as in any sport and that is LUCK. The *rub of the green* as we say here.

Surprise Surprise!

Speaking of luck, let me give you a perfect example or two just to prove how important it is to have that all-important bit of luck on your side.

A couple of Saturdays ago I was reading my Irish Field racing paper as I always do on Saturday afternoons. In one of the preview pages of the week-end race meetings, there was a picture of a horse which the headline on the page referred to as a potential winner for the following day Sunday in Gowran Park. The caption underneath the picture read: "Following his recent success in Leopardstown he is expected to make it two in a row at Gowran tomorrow". I proceeded to have a look at the actual race card for Gowran and checked the form and breeding of the horse pictured. To my astonishment I realised that this horse was the son of the black mare which I had picked out in Goffs four years earlier and the one that Marc and Jay reckoned I might have problems with because of her temperament, remember?! I thought to myself: 'Jesus, don't tell me this horse could have been the one after all' and wouldn't you know it, Surprise, Sur-*fucking*-prise, he had won three races to-date and was well-fancied to win again tomorrow. His current prize money won was €51,000 for win and place money. If this wasn't bad enough, I looked up the website to see if he was sold as a foal, only to find out that he was sold for €75,000 and not only that, but the mare's second foal had sold for €95,000. I thought I was seeing things and asked the man above had I done something wrong on him??? All of the annoying thoughts came into my head such as why did I not follow my instincts, why did I look at her as the very first viewing, why did I listen to the lads etc. I know in hindsight it was easy to say I was right and everyone else was wrong, but you see that's the 'luck' I'm talking about. If my luck was in I'd have bought that mare that day but such is life, especially in the horseracing game. I had often wondered how that mare had turned out for who bought her and was kind of afraid to check it out but of all the horses to be pictured on the Irish Field, they would choose the one I didn't want to look up. Mind you, on the Sunday morning I paid a visit to the bookies and checked what price he was and he was 9 to 1 morning price. I had to have €50 on him to win even just for interest and guess what he fucking won again. Even though I won €450 on my bet, I still didn't know whether to laugh or cry. Of course, I told Jay and Marc all about him and what could they say only – *Shite!* The horse is now a five year old and the mare's second foal also won at 3 years so all-in-all somebody else got to live my dream on this occasion. I purposely haven't used the names of the horses in question simply they belong to someone else and anyway they put me in bad form!! Now wouldn't you think that all of this would be enough for me to finally throw in the towel and realise that it just wasn't meant to be for me. Well, I have to say that it did hit me for six and made me wonder what I had to do to have a bit of luck. To think of all the hassle I'd had with my horses during those interim years while the first mare I looked at and wanted had so much success!! Need I say anymore? Jay did say to me however that had we bought the mare it may not have worked out the same which I suppose is true to a certain extent so no point crying over it now anyway! Life goes on.

The foal sales in Goffs was fast approaching and the Tattersalls sales was even a week before that so we were extremely busy getting the foals ready. I must have walked ten miles a day teaching them how to walk and get used to being handled etc. It was hard to know what to expect from the upcoming sales however as was the case with all businesses in what was now a very, very serious economic downturn. I should know, I still haven't found a permanent job. The results from sales that had already taken place in recent weeks both here and abroad had shown a substantial decline in numbers sold and prices acquired. There was however plenty of money around for the top class stock. I'm not sure whether any of the foals which I was walking fell into this category but Jay was adamant that the Elusive Quality foal certainly did.

Well, the weeks flew by and before we knew it we were off to Tattersalls for the National Hunt sales for foals. Marc and Jay had been to Kentucky for the week prior to the sales and I had looked after the mares and foals while they were away. I was glad when they got back I can tell you. They arrived home on the morning of the sales and Jay had to go to college so a sleepy Marc came with me to the sales which is a good hour-and-a-half drive from home. The only National Hunt foal they had was particularly well-bred and she was the daughter of a Cheltenham winner so it was difficult to say just what she was worth. She wasn't entering the sales ring until the following day and we would spend today just showing her to prospective buyers. When the foal arrived at the sales complex she was nervous enough and was difficult enough to handle for the first few hours. Marc wasn't long waking up because of her antics. We spent the whole day leading here in and out of the stable and walking her around for a hell of a lot of viewers. By the time darkness fell she was quiet as a mouse and we were fit for one place only and that was the couch. Marc slept all the way home in the jeep and I had the radio on full blast in case I did. We went to bed early and set off again at 6am the following day.

The lot number given to the foal meant that she would not enter the sales ring until the afternoon, but we had to be there early for any more viewers and again there were plenty of them. I said to Marc at one stage while I was out of breath from walking that if this foal doesn't make a good price, they may throw their hat at it.

'You just never know', he replied.

The sales were on in earnest at this point and the general opinion was that trade was way down on previous years and that the recession was definitely taking its' toll. The number of foals not being sold or being literally given away was soul-destroying for those who had put so much time and money into having them there in the first place. There was the very odd one who was maybe related to a major winner or from a top-class sire/mare who was making good money, but they were few and far between. The one we had, however, was particularly well-bred and a lovely-looking foal, so we had to be hopeful. Having walked for hours on end, the time eventually came and the hip numbers were placed on the filly foal and we gave her a brush-down to have her looking her best and off I headed with her to the pre-parade ring, just to take in another few laps before she entered the actual sales ring. As I walked her around, various people asked me to take her out for them to examine her closely. By the time it was her turn to go in, I was wrecked and hoped that the filly was walking better than I was at this stage. She did behave perfectly though, so I was delighted with her. This was all very new to such a young horse. Into the ring and the auctioneer is shouting at pace to get the bidding off to a start. The bids eventually took off and came hard and fast as far as €28,000, at which point they began to slow down substantially. €35,000 was the last bid, but the lads had decided that this would not be enough to let her go. It's a lot of money to turn down, I remember thinking and bird-in-the-hand and all that, but it wasn't up to me, I was only helping out. We brought the foal back home and she may re-visit the sales as a yearling or be placed in training, so as is the case with young horses, it's too early to say. A lot of work, an awful lot of work for nothing to this point, I thought to myself. Like most things in business life, things are never as easy and straight-forward as you would like them to be.

Goffs Again

Another week and four more foals to be brought to the flat sales in Goffs. All of the preparatory work done. Lots more showing and walking to be done prior to the actual sales. Two foals to be sold on the Wednesday and two more on the Friday, which means a full week's work between getting them there, showing them, looking after them and eventually selling them, hopefully. Bear in mind the economic downturn will have much the same effect here as it did last week at the National Hunt sales. Bear in mind also that in a few weeks time A Chuisle goes into the horses-in-training sales and for lower grade horses at this point in time it's not looking too positive. All I can do is hope for the best for now.

Monday morning 6am and we're off again. The two foals for the Wednesday sale are with us this morning and we will show them for two days prior to their turn. The actual sales begin on Tuesday and as is the case in most thoroughbred sales, the best are kept till last, so the really expensive types won't be sold till Friday and the two we have with us today will be somewhere in the middle, although the lads are not expecting too much for these two, mainly because they are from a cheapish stallion. The Elusive Quality and the other American-bred foal will go in on the big day Friday.

When we arrived at Goffs, we got the two foals settled and decided to go for some breakfast, just in case it got very busy with lookers. We had a full breakfast and just as well we did, as from the time we returned to the stables we had people calling to see them. I suppose in recessionary times there will always be the cute *hoors* looking for the up-turn and re-sell. Then there are the people who just could not afford to invest in a racehorse in the good times for the trade, so this effectively made for a buyers market. Looking at some of the low prices for some very well-bred horses, it was a good time to buy if you were in a position to do so. Well, I think it was anyway, although time will tell. I know that I for one had I the facility and the money to keep them, would have bought five or six foals for the price of one and taken the chance that one of them would turn a profit as a yearling, when things may be a lot better. Buying foals and re-selling them as yearlings is known as *pin-hooking*, so my opinion was that this may well have been a pin-hooker's paradise. I look forward to the returns from next year's yearling sales, to see if I'm correct. The cheap stock would be available for the first few days and maybe even the odd one on the Friday. We stayed at the sales till dark at which time we headed home having been very surprised at how many lookers we'd had. This doesn't always mean that they will sell well or even sell, but it is better than nobody looking. Early to bed and 6am Tuesday morning we're on the road again. I never worked as hard until I gave up work. Think about it!!!

Tuesday was the first day of the sales, although the two we brought were not in until Wednesday. Again, we were extremely busy, considering. My predictions of bad prices and high numbers of unsold stock however were spot-on, as day one for vendors was a complete disaster. Only 28% of those who entered the ring on day one actually sold and even at that, the prices were extremely low for some. Back to my buyers market reference. Most vendors would have been delighted just to make enough to clear the stallion fees, not to mention make a profit. Well, no matter what, this is the way things are at present, so all any business can do is struggle on and hope for the best. Home again on Tuesday evening, having walked for Ireland again all day, early to bed and Wednesday morning 6am, we're on the road again.

As I said earlier, the two we had for sale today were only mediocre, as the stallion's progeny to-date were not exactly setting the horse-racing world alight and this particular stallion had covered a lot of mares, so breeders were actually competing against themselves and only the really well-bred ones from the mares' side or the exceptional lookers were selling at all. Both of ours were by the same stallion and one of them had a very well-bred dam, while the other one was only ok and on top of this he was a *box-walker*. A box-walker is a term used for a horse who for some reason when they are put in their stable/box, they walk around and around in circles for the length of time they are awake in the box. It is a very annoying mental disorder of some sort in any horse and very off-putting for buyers once the auctioneer mentions it, which he is obliged to do once the vendor informs the sales office, which he/she is obliged to do.

So the hours are flying by and the first foal (the boxwalker) is in failry quickly to the sales ring. He was actually a very nice-looking horse and perfect in every way other than the box-walking. I led him into the ring and the auctioneer shouted 'Here we have a very nice colt foal from the family of' (whoever it was on his pedigree). 'He has been known to *box-walk*, so who'll start the bidding?' It's funny when you actually sell a horse at public auction, such as Goffs or Tattersalls etc. that the one thing you wish for in the sales ring is the shout of the spotters. These are the boys or girls who are positioned around the ring facing the audience and taking the bids as they come, at which stage, the

Spotter shouts really loud something like 'YO!', so as a seller you want to hear as many loud 'YO's!' as you can and as a buyer you just want to hear one 'YO!' from you own bid. As soon as 'box-walker' was mentioned, there wasn't a 'YO!' in the house for this foal however and so I led him back out without a single bid. There were many more foals brought out without a 'YO!', mind you and not just box-walkers. There are ways of dealing with this condition by the way, but it would take me too long to explain.

The second foal we had that day would be entered for sale in a couple more hours time, so I went and got a coffee and a chocolate bar, brought them back to outside the stable and sat on a bale of hay and enjoyed them. Ah, this is the life! I thought to myself, sitting on a bale of hay having coffee and a bar in the fresh air, selling horses for other people. It may not be as secure as the 9 to 5 office job I left, but by God it was definitely healthier. Maybe I was just clutching at straws – or hay even, to keep myself positively motivated while out of work, I don't know, but for some reason it felt good to be free.

The next foal, by the way, was the one who was my favourite and the one I would have loved to have been able to buy for Jay and I to put in training. Unfortunately, until I get sorted with a job and A Chuisle, I couldn't, but I will follow his racing career with great interest from here on. The time eventually came for him to go to the ring. One man who studied him a few times during the days prior was particularly fond of him and he was a really lovely man who was fairly old and I was hoping that if anybody bought this little fella that it would be him. I'm not exactly sure what it was about this foal, but he was just a grand, genuine little horse. I told the old man and man's son this when I showed him to them.

Into the ring we go and after a few minutes there's a loud 'YO!', followed by a few more, bringing the price to €10,000. In the circumstances, this was a decent enough price. As I led him out of the ring and back to the stable, I wondered who had bought him. Much to my delight, after a few minutes the man and his son called to the stable and said to me: 'I hope you're right about him being a nice horse, as we've just bought him'. I wished them luck and after a few minutes they were off to make arrangements to have the foal collected. I gave the foal a pat on the neck and wished him all the best also and as I said earlier, I will be keeping a close eye on his progress. Time for a quick cuppa before we loaded up the one who didn't sell and off home. I went to collect the unsold foal to load and a couple of lads were from another stud farm and asked how much we'd let him go for. Marc asked them to make an offer and after about twenty minutes dealing, the foal was sold for a small amount. Not sure what the lads will do with him, but good luck to them. He could very well turn out to be a very nice horse, so we'll see what happens. So it was off home with an empty horse-box. Everyone happy enough.

Jay had arranged a few days off from college so that he would be there to show and take charge of the two American-bred foals, which were being brought up on Thursday morning. He got the train home on Wednesday night and was up at the crack of dawn and gone with Marc with the foals in tow by 6am. I was glad of the lie-on at this stage and would follow them up later on to give them a hand during the day.

I've never seen Jay and Marc as nervously excited about two foals before. I suppose having gone to Kentucky for the first time and spent a lot of Eamon's money on the two mares was enough to make anyone nervous. Anyway, here they are today with the results of their venture in the form of two extremely well-bred colt foals. Two colts alone was a brilliant return thus far. What were they worth though?? Who knows? With the way things are at the minute it is anybody's guess. Having said that, they are worth a lot of money on paper, one of them in particular. They were being sold on the best day of the sales and a lot of the major players in the game were around.

From the minute the lads arrived at Goffs, there was a line of people waiting for them. It was hard to know whether it was just lookers to see what the American stock was like, or whether it was people who were genuinely interested in buying. Either way, the foals had to be shown properly to anybody who asked to see them. I didn't arrive until 11am and by that time the two lads were red in the face, having walked so much on what was a cool winter morning. They were relieved to see me and straight away there were orders for tea and bottles of *Lucozade* and fajita wraps etc. Only the best for our Jay. No such thing as a ham or cheese sandwich with our man. Fajita wraps you know! 'It's far from fajita wraps you were reared' says I, but on I went with the shopping list. When I got back, the two lads had hardly enough time to sit down and enjoy their break, such was the interest in the foals.

The first of these two would enter the ring around lunch-time on Friday, so considering there was still a full day to go before the sales, it was extremely busy with the number of people looking at this early stage on the previous day. Jay said a few times that by the time the second foal (which was the one most were interested in) sold,he would be wrecked from all the walking. I told him that if the foal didn't make a very good price that his life wouldn't be worth living anyway.

'Jeasus, don't say that!' says Marc 'I'm nervous enough as it is'.

The three of us had a good laugh at this. Well, all joking aside, I tried to re-assure the lads that if even a handful of the large number of lookers want to buy the foals, well then you can't lose. As soon as one person would finish viewing the foals and just as they were brought back to the stable door, another person or two would arrive. I do emphasise that even though it was hard work on the lads, there was nobody complaining that there was so much interest. Thursday continued as it had started until darkness fell around 5pm, at which time it was time for a well-earned rest for both man and beast. The foals were fed and watered for the night and God help them, they devoured their food and both were lying down within minutes, at which time we hit the road home. I can tell you that as soon as Jay was fed, it was only a few minutes before he was lying down also when he did get home.

Eventually the day of reckoning was upon us and before I even awoke on Friday morning, both Jay and Marc were in Goffs. I think their adrenalin was working overtime. I followed them later that morning and on arrival again this time approx 9:30am both the lads were walking up and down, showing the foals and had been continuously from around 7.30am. They each took staggered breaks and I filled in while they were away. In the hour while the two lads had breakfast, I and whoever was with me, never stopped for a minute. Well, it was so busy that the time just flew by and before we knew it, it was time for the first foal to be brushed up and have his lot number placed on his hips and ready to enter the pre-parade ring. The expectation levels, following so much interest and the fact that these were two very nice foals, were high. The first one we didn't really know what to expect, as the sire/father was very new to Europe and didn't have any runners here to-date, but the second one had sired Raven's Pass among other winners, so that was a major plus on his page.

Time for Jay and the first one to enter the sales ring. 'Next up, we have Lot No. 1085, a smashing son of Pleasantly Perfect, from Fortbarrington Stud, who'll start me off?' said the auctioneer. This was a young April foal and he was an absolute beaut. My only fear was that of the unknown and I wondered if buyers would be willing to take the chance on looks and pedigree alone, without information from the track on runners to-date from the same family. The bidding was brisk but not frantic, however. The auctioneer was flying as far as twenty thousand, but it slowed considerably thereafter. The final bid would be twenty-eight thousand euros, but because of the quality of this foal, this would not be enough, so unfortunately to an extent, he would not be changing hands today. I say 'unfortunately to an extent', quite simply because just because he didn't sell today didn't mean that he was surplus to requirements to bring home. Far from it, this was still a cracker of a horse who will either be sold as a yearling, or will go into training and was far too good to sell for what was small money for this quality.

The lads were a little disappointed after all of their hard work in getting him to the sales looking so well and showing him for two days non-stop. Yet they were still very positive that they still had him and that he was a nice one to have regardless.

'Not to worry' I told Jay 'your number one will make up for it'.

'Hope you're right, Da!'

Eamon, Marc and Jay were always of the opinion that the Elusive Quality foal was the one in any case, so it was all down to him later on. The viewers were still calling in large numbers and would continue to do so, right up to the time of sale. It wasn't long before that time did come around, at which stage the butterflies were eating the belly out of the lads. I remember holding the foal as they carried out the final touches on his presentation for the sales ring, their hands were shaking and they were a bundle of nerves the pair of them. Everything ready and in fairness to Marc and Jay, they deserve all the credit in the world on how each of the foals were presented for sale. This one in particular was a very striking individual, with a colour somewhere between bay and chestnut, with a couple of white socks and a white blaze on his face. He was so big and strong for his age and towards each of the others, that you could tell in a glance that he was something special. Well, whatever we all thought of him regardless, it was now time to see what all of the experts thought. As Jay led him to the pre-parade ring, he caught the eye of every person he passed along the way, with his ears pricked and his commanding steps, almost like a fully-grown horse. When it was time to bring him to the sales ring, I walked down the chute behind him and Jay, just in case he made any fuss. He was a little nervous, but behaving very well in all. The person leading him, I think was even more nervous. Jay stood him in the waiting area beside the ring, as they waited for the previous lot number to finish. The foal stood big and proud at this point, as though he was showing off. He just looked magnificent. At long last, here we go.

'OK, ladies and gentlemen, lot no. 1139, here's one of the ones we were all waiting for' the auctioneer announced. 'The only foal in the sale by the already-famous Elusive Quality, of the one-and-only Raven's Pass, at such an early stage in his stallion career. Look at the page, look at the walk, need I say anymore? Who'll start me off?'

'Forty thousand? Thirty? Twenty?'

'Twenty I have, thank you, sir'.

'Twenty-five, thirty, thirty-five, who'll give me Forty, Forty I have'.

'Keep looking at the walk all the time, ladies and gentlemen, here we have a proper racehorse. From the sire of Raven's pass, I tell you'.

'Forty-five, Fifty, Fifty-five.'

Lowering his voice, he almost whispers: 'This fellow could be yours today. He's here to sell and I'll say it again. Look at the walk, let there be no doubts, here we have a cracking individual, who ticks all the right boxes'.

'Sixty thousand, I have'.

Jay in the ring, walking at pace for what must seem like an eternity to him and the bidding is fairly fast and furious. The spotters' 'YO's!' are coming from every angle to this point and as Jay passes me by, I'm standing in the pit beside the ring, he throws a little grin as much as to say 'I told ya, Da!'

'Sixty-five' and straight away 'YO!'

'Seventy, I have. The bid is on my right, Seventy-Five thousand, he's still cheap, you know, lads'.

'Eighty thousand. OK, ladies and gentlemen, it's time to get serious for what you and I know will be a serious racehorse. Eighty-five.'

'Eighty-five around the ring. Ninety thousand, back to you, sir. If you want him, you may go again, sir, I'm afraid'.

'Ninety-five thousand. Have one more look at the walk before you decide'.

'One Hundred Thousand Euro, thank you very much. Is that it?'

'One Hundred Thousand around the ring once, twice, I have the hammer ready.'

'YO!'

'One Hundred and Five Thousand, I'm bid'.

Jay is fit to collapse, so am I and I'm only watching. Marc is so relieved, having spent so much on the mare that at this stage he's almost oblivious to what's going on.

'One Hundred and Five Thousand once, twice and around the ring for the last time, the hammer's up.'

Bang!

'Thank you very much, sir, you've just bought a nice horse'.

I met Jay as he exited the ring and the adrenalin had kicked in and he was thrilled skinny that the foal he hadn't shut up about since his first trip to Kentucky where they bought the mare carrying him, had just proved him right and had sold for what was an absolutely brilliant price, particularly under the current economic climate within the trade and indeed all businesses.

'I told ya, Da, wasn't I right!'

'Fair play to you, Jay, you were spot on'.

This was the gist of our conversation as we brought the foal back to the stable.

'I'll be glad to sit down, Da'.

I told him he could relax now and enjoy the remainder of the sales. The new owner arrived shortly afterwards and after all the congratulations and handshakes, it was time to say goodbye to the Elusive Quality and relax for a while and enjoy the sales before heading for home. Jay put his arm around the foal's neck in a touching embrace and whispered into his ear:

'Good luck, little fella, see you in the winner's enclosure'.

Needless to say, his progress from here on will be monitored closely. I can guarantee you now that whatever happens and wherever this foal ends up or runs, or whatever our Jay will be first to know such is his love and interest of thorough-bred bloodstock.

We now had time for a break and a celebratory cuppa and we could also study the remainder of the catalogue to see what lots were still to come etc. History would be made in today's sales as the only progeny from the famous and much-loved racehorse George Washington would sell later in the evening. When I say the only progeny I mean the one and only foal, a filly, which he ever fathered. 'Gorgeous George' as he was commonly known, was deemed infertile at stud, but from all the mares he had covered, just one somehow was pregnant. Talk about a stroke of luck for one breeder. What was she worth?? A small fortune, I and everybody else reckoned. She was due into the ring in a couple of hours time, so the interest levels grew with great anticipation. Jay in particular enjoyed the rest and he'd had such a busy few days at the sales, that he never even got to see the George Washington filly foal. We went to where she was stabled and when we got there she was being shown to someone else, as was the case all day, I presume. We had a look and it was special to see the one and only foal that George would ever have. A gorgeous little chestnut filly with the same white blaze as her father before her. It was only an hour or so afterwards that she entered the ring and as expected the place lit up. The spotters had been shouting 'YO!' at every available opportunity all week, but this one would make them hoarse. Amidst all the shouting and excitement, this little filly foal walked around with not a clue what all the fuss was about and the auctioneer quickly moved from one hundred thousand to two hundred thousand, to three hundred thousand, to finally bringing down the hammer at three hundred and eighty thousand euros. Here's hoping she turns out to be a bargain and keeps on the family name and tradition, if only just for poor old George, who left us all far too soon, following a tragic accident while racing in the Breeder's Cup in America.

Back to
the Real World

With the sales over for another year, it was back to reality for me. The sales had given me a great boost for the week and I never even listened to the doom and gloom of job losses and credit crunch which was news headlines all over the world by now. I'm not saying I didn't care or wasn't concerned, particularly being out of work, but it was nice just to get away from it all for a while. The next sales I had to attend however may not give me the same boost I need. Goresbridge mixed sale for all sorts of horses and mainly those at the very bottom of the market. Not a very nice place to be right now. As I said earlier, I was just cutting my losses at this point with A Chuisle and hoping to get enough just to pay off any outstanding bills even.

I decided to go to Goresbridge as I was advised that without a winning mare or at least a very well-related mare, there wasn't much point in going to Goffs, where the entry fee was high enough for a lower-grade horse. The minimum bid in Goffs however is two thousand euros, but as I said, at the present time, with lower-grade stock two thousand is even too much to expect. So off to Goresbridge, Co. Kilkenny in the hope of finding a buyer for A Chuisle. She was always a lovely-looking filly, perfectly correct etc. but just didn't have the all-important winning evidence in her CV. She was perfect for breeding, for National Hunt racing and so on, but for me just at the minute, she was surplus to requirements unfortunately. It was time to be realistic and sell her on to clear my bills.

Goresbridge is a small, picturesque village on the outskirts of Kilkenny. An area steeped in horse-racing tradition and very close to some very famous racing trainers and not far from Gowran Park racecourse. The sales complex is in the old cattle mart site. It is a nice country setting and well worth a visit. The mixed sales today had a variety of horses, from foals to breeding stock, to horses in and out of training etc. The first lot was due in the ring at 1pm, so we left home for the one-hour trip at around eleven, having loaded A Chuisle in the box and fed the other horses. I had no illusions of making money or expecting a big profit or anything of the sort. As a result, we were very relaxed and looked forward to a day out and nothing more.

When we got there, it was extremely quiet and to be honest for the times we have, I remember saying to Jay and Marc:

'Will be bother bringing her in?'

They just laughed and said:

'Weill ya come on you mad eejit, we didn't come down here just to turn around and go back'.

'Fair enough' says I and off we went to the stabling area.

Jay led A Chuisle in and settled her into the stable and it was bloody freezing, so I treated the lads to a full Irish breakfast and A Chuisle to a bale of hay, which cost me a fiver by the way. I would've nearly got her a breakfast for that!!! The full Irish warmed us up at least and after a few cups of tea, it was back to the stable in case anyone wanted to see here before the sale. A few people did have a look, mind you, so I was hoping they'd start a bidding war between them when she went into the ring. We had a nice, early lot number, so we would know our fate within an hour or so. Not too bad! A Chuisle has always had a habit of getting a bit on her toes when it comes to public gatherings where other horses also appear. She was the same at the races for instance. This meant that prior to racing as in this case being auctioned, the person looking after her had their hands full during the preliminaries. Today this was Jay's job and I can tell you that it takes a good horseman to manage a racehorse when they become excited for whatever reason. Jay did a great job, although on a few occasions he called her a few names which I won't repeat. Eventually she walked into the small sales ring, which is very nicely laid out with the seats very close by. When I say she walked in, it was more like she exploded into the ring, as she was so excited and Jay was at his very best to manage her. I forgot to mention that the sales so far had been diabolical and no horses were selling. Anyway, we were here now, so let's see what happens. She skipped around the ring and the auctioneer did his best to point out her best features and Jay did his best to hold on to her and I did my best not kick myself for getting into this situation in the first place and Marc did his best to keep warm and while we were all doing our best the buyers were doing their worst and to make a long story short, it was a complete waste of time and when Jay got back to the stable he was sweating and nearly ate both me and the horse for what had just been the longest hour-and-a-half of his life. We loaded her up straight away and headed for home.

'What will we do with her now, lads?' I asked.

Jay, with the red face, replied:

'Da, you can do what ya feckin' like with her, but don't ever ask me to lead her around a sales ring again'.

All we could do was laugh, to be honest. We brought her home, fed her up and then went and fed ourselves. We'd put the thinking caps back on tomorrow.

My thinking cap is worn out from horses right now. For the next few days I put a cover on A Chuisle and let her out each day to the paddock thanks to Eamon and I fed her up and put her in each night. Indeed she was minded like a child and all the time I wondered what to do with her. I wrote earlier about the oversupply problem in Irish racing at present at the bottom end of the market and I had no intention of adding to it by breeding from her as a result. I could build her up for a few months now that she is growing so well etc. and maybe she'd be good enough to pick up a race in the spring/summer National Hunt campaign. However, I had no room for maybe's in my head at present, so I was at a loss as to what would come of her.

On a Friday night mid-December, my mobile rang and a man asked me:

'Did you ever get rid of the Kalanisi filly?'

I said no and asked who I was speaking to. The man was from Cork and had looked at her at the sales and indeed had spoken to me and left phone numbers between us etc. which I'd forgotten about. I remembered him when he mentioned that he was interested in her for show-jumping at his homeplace for his daughter to use for practice. I asked him if he wanted to buy her now and he told me that with the way things are that I would never sell her for what she's worth, but he said:

'If you like, I'll give you a few bob for luck and I promise she would be well-looked after'.

I told him I would think about it, thanked him for the offer and said I'd let him know. Time to put the cap on again!!

So here's the scenario: I have a four-year old filly who has cost me a lot of money to this point. I have given her every chance in training. On the flat at two, three and four years old and over hurdles twice at four. She was not good enough to win on the flat in Ireland and has shown some potential over the jumps in the sense that she was a good jumper and given time she might pick up a race somewhere along the line. She is still costing me for keep and taking up a lot of my time during the winter months. The trade is at an all-time low, so I can't sell her. I either keep her, not knowing what for and I'm not forgetting that "they shoot horses, don't they" or I can literally give her away to a Corkman who wants her as a show-jumping pet. My thinking cap has a hole in the top of it and I am in a very strict frame of mind right now to face up to reality. On weighing up my options, I decide to cut my losses and take up the Corkman's offer. I rang him back there and then and agreed to deliver the horse to him the following Tuesday. All the lads agreed with me that it was the best thing to do. I was comfortable with my decision and the following Tuesday I borrowed the jeep and horsebox from Marc and I drove all the way to Cork, where I said goodbye to the filly who had occupied my mind and my dreams for four years and who, even though she was not good enough to win, held a very special place in my heart. Horse-racing ownership is not really a place for sentimentality however so it was time for me to move on. Was this the end of the dream?? I suppose the fact that now I had no horses would certainly have a huge bearing on me ever having a winner, but I was in a positive state of mind and with Christmas just around the corner, I decided to enjoy the break from worrying over what to do with horses, from working in all sorts of weathers in looking after them, from trying to keep the bills paid to keep them and just enjoy the break in general. I'm still looking for a permanent job, but the few bob redundancy allows me not to worry too much for now, even though things were really at an all-time low in the economy, but as far as I'm concerned I've been here before and the only way is up. Once I get sorted again, I'll review the situation and hopefully horse number whatever it is will keep the dream alive for me. I'm now on my way back from Cork with a few bob luck money in my pocket from a very nice man whose last words to me on leaving were:

'Keep the chin up, young fella and what's for you won't pass you by'/

Strangely enough, I'd only heard that saying once before and it had been many years ago, but for some reason, it lodged in my brain for the full journey home and is still there today, as a kind of comforting factor to me in uncertain times.

Christmas Break

Need I say it, regardless of what's happening in the world, my other half has the tickets arranged for the four of us to head off for the Christmas. The cases are packed for the past week, we are all under strict instructions to have whatever clothes we need washed left out and don't leave anything to the last minute. Check the passports that they are not expired, is my job. Jesus, come to think of it, I better check them today. Fair play to her though, in fairness. This year's Christmas dinner will be had in, would you believe, Dubai, of all places. I've never been, needless to say and am really looking forward to it. Herself has it booked for ages and as a result saved a fortune towards today's prices to get there. The hotel looks out of this world and she saved a lot on it also. As a matter of fact, with the amount of planning my wife puts into going away each Christmas, it works out almost cheaper to do so, what with all the expense at home. Not saying this is why we go, but it's nice to know. We all love to head off somewhere exciting at this time of year. I personally find it gives me something to look forward to. I much prefer the excitement of the whole new experience, rather than stuffing my face with food in front of the telly at home for a week or more. I also find it gives the body and mind a great boost on returning home and facing a new year with a positive attitude. I told them at home the other night that when I'm in Dubai, I might try contact Sheikh Mohammed to see if he has any nice horses for sale. Vera and Erica together shouted:

'Don't you mention horses over the Christmas!'

Jay and I had a good laugh at same. Actually speaking of Sheikh Mohammed, I had the pleasure of visiting Kildangan Stud with Marc and Eamon last week. Kildangan is a famous, world-renowned stud owned by Sheikh Mohammed. It is only a short drive from home for us and we went to see the stallions on show for next year, which Marc had arranged. Marc and Jay had bought a new mare for Eamon on their latest visit to Kentucky and when she has the foal she is carrying, soon afterwards she will visit a stallion for next year's mating. The lads had specific stallions in mind for her and subject to viewing, it would more than likely be one from Kildangan which we were about to see in the flesh. Talk about top horses and big names from the track! All I could say was Wow! Added to the horses standing here was the very beauty of the place. This stud farm is without doubt one of the most impressive stud farms in the world. Set in the prime pastures of Co.Kildare, it is quite simply breath-taking. I'd been here a few times before and Jay had worked there with the mares as work experience during his transition year in school, so I knew what to expect, but for anybody visiting for the first time, it is just a jewel in the crown of Irish racing bloodstock and this is even before we see any horses. We wait in the plush surrounds of the office, where a young fella called Eamon greets us and brings us to the stallion stabling area.

First for viewing was *Teofilo*. When the young handler led him into the yard, my first impressions were wow! what a giant of a horse and indeed what an absolute gorgeous horse. Teofilo had an unblemished record as a two-year old as he was unbeaten in all his runs including group one victories in the National Stakes and in an unforgettable Dewhurst Stakes, in which the epic battle between him and Coolmore's *Holy Roman Emperor* took place with Teofilo victorious by the narrowest of margins. The two Irish horses well clear of the remainder, showing just how good each of them were. Unfortunately, Teofilo was not to grace the racing world with his presence as a three-year old, due to some sort of injury set-back. Such a pity, as he was undoubtedly a true champion and the son of the famous Gallileo will prove himself further as a champion stallion in the future, if his looks and pedigree are anything to go by. We'll have to wait and see and hopefully pending on the lads' decision today, I might even get to see one of his sons or daughters born and reared in Fortbarrington.

Next up was the now famous stallion *Cape Cross*, winner of a couple of group one races himself and a hugely successful stallion over the last few years. You would know straight away that he is getting on in years at this stage, but he still looks like the true successful horse that he is. He is sire of lots and lots of great winners, but the one that sticks out most of all and a personal favourite of mine being a filly, has to be *Ouija Board*. Twice winner of the Breeder's Cup fillies and mares race, not to mention her achievements in both UK and Ireland. She was indeed a once-in-a-lifetime-type filly and one who really put her father's name firmly on the top of sires' lists. Eamon then told us that the next one we'd see would be *Authorized* and to me, this was the type of day I absolutely loved. I felt like a young child in a famous sweet shop. I had watched all of these horses during their racing careers and never did I think that I would ever get the opportunity to meet them in person, so to speak. This was the top of the ladder, the cream of the crop and although I was a million miles away from the top in my journey to date in the racing world, it was just magic to see these famous animals in the flesh. Authorized, an Epsom Derby winner, was followed by *Shirocco*, a group one winner in different countries , followed by *Kheleyf*, a leading sire of two-year old winners from his first crop, followed by *Ramonti*, who had won as far away as Hong Kong and also won the Sussex and Lochinge in the UK.

'Ah Lads' says I to Marc: 'Is there any end to them?', at which stage young Eamon says:

'Now we have Ravens' Pass, just back from his Breeder's Cup triumph in America'.

Jesus, I couldn't believe it. I had forgotten that Ravens' Pass was even standing for stud duties in Kildangan. Here in the flesh was the son of Elusive Quality, who my Jay had never shut up about, due to the foal whom I mentioned so much of earlier. I remember using the camera on my phone to show Jay the photos as unfortunately he couldn't be with us today. I knew he would love to have seen them all, but Ravens' Pass in particular. I even video'd him as he walked up and down the yard for us to view. To be honest, I didn't even take much notice of what he looked like, because as far as I was concerned, this was Ravens' Pass, full stop. I said to the lads:

'Do you mind telling me, how in the name of God can you decide which stallion to bring the mare to?'

Marc tried to explain to me that there are certain calculations and considerations to be brought into the scenario and also mentioned that just as is the case in owning a racehorse you also need luck.

'Rather you than me deciding' I said.

'These stallions don't come cheap, you know, pardon the pun!'

Anyway, that was that and while the lads were left to ponder which stallion to use, I was left with a very special memory of a lovely visit to Kildangan Stud, just outside Athy, owned by Sheikh Mohammed of Dubai. When I see him next week, I'll let him know how much I enjoyed it!!! The sheer quality of the horses I'd just been shown added to the sheer beauty of the facility, made this a truly special day out for me.

Later that evening I rang Jay and told him where I'd spent the afternoon.

'I knew the lads were going there today, but didn't know you were going with them, Da' he said, 'You must have enjoyed it, I'm delighted you went 'cause I didn't get the chance to tell you that they were going out today'.

'What did you think of Ravens' Pass' was his first question.

I told him I was so excited having heard the name from him so often that I didn't really study him, but rather just watched him in awe, following all the conversations we'd had about him during the season, including the texts while I was in Prague.

'You're a right lad to send to view a stallion' says Jay.

I laughed at his remark and explained that I was only there as an observer.

'Which one was your favourite' he asked.

'Not sure really, but if I had to narrow it down to one, I'd probably go with Teofilo' was my answer.

'Time will tell' said Jay and we said we'd talk more when he was home at the week-end. What a few weeks it's been for me on the horse front. I've gone from trying to get rid of a horse that nobody wanted in the racing world of today, to viewing horses that everybody wanted in their pedigrees, all in the space of these few weeks. It was a type of confusing time if you get my drift, but I got to thinking that it just about sums up bloodstock and racing in general at the current time. Put simply, and my words are backed up by all of the recent end-of-year sales results, the bottom end of the market is now gone completely and unless the horse is from the top end, then nobody wants them. I alluded to overproduction in the industry earlier and how something needed to be done about it. Now in a recessionary climate it will probably sort itself out in the sense as in most businesses today that people cannot afford to throw good money after bad anymore. In racing/breeding, this will result in a lot of mares not being covered this year and maybe next and maybe even never again. There will be a reduction in ownership at the lower end and I imagine that the number of syndicates will also reduce. What will all of this mean to the industry, is the question on everybodys' lips. Well, I'm no expert and never pretended to be, but one thing I do know is that I have experienced the bottom end of the market and for the moment I am glad to be away from it during these uncertain times and while it has put a severe dent in my quest to own a winner, I do have to face reality for the moment. No point flogging a dead horse! I've been tempted to buy one while prices are so low and if I was in a new job right now, who knows I may have But for now I'm sitting back and waiting and taking a break. Not that my non-involvement in race-horse ownership will be front-page news or anything, but right now I've a feeling that many more people are in the same boat and this could well be front-page news on racing tabloids for months to come. Horse-racing is no different from any other industry at the end of the day and no doubt there will be lots of casualties by the time this whole economy collapse and credit-crunch (today's buzz-words) are sorted out. How did things get so bad so fast all over the world? In my opinion it was all down to mismanagement in the world-wide banking systems and as a result nobody allowed for the rainy day, which has now arrived in buckets. However, such is life and this doom and gloom collapse story is for experts to write about. In the meantime I'm off to Dubai for ten days, recession or not and by the time I get back maybe things will look a bit better and before long there'll be good news in general and I'll be in a better position to get back in the game. The Sheikhs in racing send their horses to Dubai for the winter-time back home and by the time the horses return to race in Irish and English spring/summers they'll have had the sun on their backs and be full of life. Hopefully I'll be the same after the ten days. I can think of worse places to be, although I think it will take an awful lot more than ten days for things to pick up..

So here I am, writing beside a nice swimming pool in a Dubai hotel in 25 degree sunshine, while the news reports from home tell me it is sub-zero temperatures there. Better enjoy the last few days of sun. I started writing on a beach in Turkey in temperatures of over 30 degrees, if you remember, so all in all I've enjoyed putting pen to paper at different intervals.

If somebody had told me in Turkey that come Christmas my life would have changed so much, I'd have laughed at them then, yet I now find myself entering a new year out of work for the first time in twenty-odd years. I've taken redundancy from the 9 to 5 job, which I thought

I would retire from at sixty-five and instead of having two horses, I now have none. Looking at the positive side of things I'm financially better off than ever, but only temporarily, unless a good job comes along. I am awaiting word back on a few different jobs, but there is one in particular which I really, really want. If I am lucky enough to secure this job, I will be on the pig's back and it will only be a matter of time before I'm back in racing. That'll go down well at home! So here's hoping and I'll let you know. I'm 48 next week so January 2009 is the beginning of a whole new life for me. I have every intention of embracing 2009 in a confident state of mind, so onwards and upwards. Somebody asked me if I had a new year's resolution the other day and I told them 'yes I have'. I told them I just want to be happy and make everybody around me even happier, to which they replied:

'What a lovely, plain, simple attitude?'

I think they were American tourists in Dubai, so I just said:

'That's me, I'm just a plain, simple sort of guy' in my best Irish accent. I think they thought I was an Irish actor or something. Yeah right, says you. Well, anyway, they thought it was amazing to meet such a down-to-earth person. God bless America. Being away for a few weeks does help take the mind off things and it is nice to do something different for a change. It's good to get away from the norm for a while and while I miss the daily updates from the Racing Post and the televised Christmas racing from Kempton and Leopardstown, it is a blessing just to forget about it for a while. Dubai has been a magical experience and with just one day left it will be sad leaving. It won't take me long, however, to catch up on the results etc. although winter racing is mainly National Hunt and while I enjoy it very much, I do have a preference for the flat. I look forward to watching a programme which was televised on Irish TV while I was away. The programme is called 'Hangin' with Hector'. Hector O'Hochagain is an Irish man from Navan in Co. Meath and you can tell from his name that he is an ambassador for our native Irish language *Gaeilge*. Hector is also the marketing face behind Irish racing with 'Let yourself go' being his catch-phrase. His programme on TV is based on spending time with famous people doing what they do and finding out about their lives. The Christmas edition happens to be Hector hanging around with trainer Aidan O'Brien and the programme was filmed during their visit to this year's Breeders' Cup in America. Hector is a type of comic character also and as a result brings a very funny and enjoyable-type aspect to his programmes yet gets the serious points across, depending on who he is meeting. Mixing the Gaelic language with English also makes for pleasant and interesting viewing. Hector also attends all of the major race meetings in Ireland and is normally to be found in some sort of marquee area as a celebrity tipster. He does the same at the annual Cheltenham festival. He has a great knowledge of Irish racing and over the years has had a few horses in training. He has a nice horse in training this year with the famous trainer in National Hunt called Noel Meade. The horse is called Steve Cappall after a famous Manchester United player, but the cappall is spelt like so, as it is the Irish name for horse. Clever one, Hector. I had the great pleasure of meeting Hector in Galway, the time Penny and Me ran there. I'd say he called me a few names actually after she lost. The day before Penny's race I went to see the Irish band *The Saw Doctors* play an open-air concert in Eyre Square in Galway city. It was a lovely, sunny afternoon and I was having a thoroughly enjoyable afternoon with my wife. I was sitting on a railing by the side of the square when I noticed a man with peaked hat down over his eyes and an anorak-type coat zipped up to the last. While I thought he was a bit over-dressed for the day that was in it, I also thought he looked very familiar and Vera said to me:

'Is this Hector walking over?' and she was spot on.

As soon as she asked me, I knew it was him for definite, even though he was dressed incognito and I don't blame him. However, as he walked past me I couldn't resist saying:

'Howya Hector' and fair play to him, he stopped and had a chat, asking me was I down for race week. I told him I had a runner on Monday evening and he was very interested in finding out about her. He was especially interested when he heard Johnny Murtagh, who is a personal friend of Hector, was booked for the ride. He asked me did I think she had a chance and I told him I was expecting a good run, so he said he'd be asking Johnny and wished me all the luck in the world and he said even if she doesn't do well, it's nice to have a runner in Galway. I thanked him, shook hands and said goodbye. Vera took a nice photo of me 'hangin' with Hector' and I have to say that he went very high in my estimation as a very nice person, because of how very polite and courteous he behaved. Fair play to you, Hector. Sorry the horse didn't win.

Luck Money
from Cork

Just as was the case with meeting Hector, some things just stay with you forever and strangely enough as I already mentioned, the man I gave A Chuisle to in Cork, for some strange reason, left a permanent mark on my brain. I cannot pinpoint exactly why, but between giving me luck money, which I wasn't expecting and using the term 'what's for you won't pass you by', there was something most unusual about him. Paddy was his first name, but other than that, I knew nothing of the man, other than that he loved horses, yet he left me feeling like Jack from the children's storybook *Jack and The Beanstalk*. Maybe it was that I'd given away the prized horse, just as Jack had given away the prized cow and where all he'd got was beans. I'd gotten a small few bob luck money. I don't know, maybe I'm just going mad and although I think that happened many years ago. Whether I was or not, I decided to see if this so-called luck money would bring me luck, so for now I had it in a special jug over the oil cooker in my kitchen. Paddy had told me that he was an ex-schoolteacher, who had taken early retirement and was in his mid-fifties. I hadn't a clue how the money might bring me luck, but it had to be something to do with horses under the circumstances. Time would tell and for now it stayed in the jug. My primary thoughts was to have the money on a horse, but I've always told everyone around me that you'll never make money backing horses and it is a dangerous game to depend on. It is a lovely, social hobby once controlled, but my advice has always been – never have your last few bob on a horse. Too many good people have suffered as a result of gambling and I know that horses can make fools out of the best of people. This so-called luck money wasn't my last few bob, but I was very much afraid of losing it on a horse, even if only for the sake of having something back from the horse, if you know what I mean. However, my mind in this case was made up and I decided to study the form as usual and wait for the right moment. I'd had nice touches over the years once I studied beforehand, rather than just betting on spec. Indeed it takes me back to one of my favourite stories in trying to back a nice winner.

When Jason was about three years old, I had a few days off from work and was minding him while my wife and daughter went somewhere. I remember that same week we'd had a lot of expenses to look after and until I got paid again at the end of the month, which was a few weeks away, money was tight to say the least and I certainly couldn't afford to throw away any on slow horses. This particular week, however, there was an excellent race meeting on at York, which included top-class races and I studied form like mad, just to see if I could find anything close to a certainty (not that there is such a thing, but you know what I mean). As I said I hadn't much spare cash, so there was no room for error and I didn't want to leave myself short of pocket money for a few weeks either, so I thought maybe I won't bother and anyway, I was baby-sitting my three-year old and could watch the racing at home.

On the Tuesday morning of that week, Vera happened to mention to me before heading off, that she'd seen a really lovely pair of boot-type sneakers, which she would love for Jay, but they were very expensive and she said she couldn't bring herself to spend that much on a child's sneakers. I said he didn't exactly need them anyway at the time and anyway, he was growing so fast, that they would be too small in no time. That morning, I brought Jay for a walk with the dog, down along the canal and fed the swans etc. which he loved to do. Even at just three, I had him mad about racing and he was a huge fan of Lester Piggott, having listened to me shouting 'Go on, Lester!' on so many occasions. My wife used say to me 'you have that child ruined. I can't even walk him to the playschool down the road, without him pretending to be Lester Piggott waiting behind me as we walk and pretending to use his whip to get up on the line to win, just as we reach the school door.' What could I say! Mind you, on our canal walk, I saw what she meant as he even had me at it. I was Pat Eddery, he was Lester and every now and then we'd take out running, with Jay doing his best running commentary, trying to sound like Peter O'Sullivan from *Channel 4*, even at three years of age. "Eddery's in front, but Piggott is going very well behind, and as they come up to the line, Piggott gets up to win" as he flew past me, slapping his backside as he passed. Sometimes I'd drive him mad by not letting him pass, which didn't go down very well. Is it any wonder he's so mad about the horses? On our way back, I picked up my Racing Post and an ice-cream for Jay in *The Pipe Shop* and when we got home, I eventually got the chance to read it, having played ball and made toasted soldiers and try to keep him out of the food cupboard etc. Today's racing from York was exceptional and the *Yorkshire Oaks* was the feature of the day, a group-one for fillies, which I really love. I decided that maybe I would call down to the bookies for an hour, having marked a few beforehand. A nice way to rear a three-year old child, says you! Jay was in his element, sitting up on the high chair with his own pen and betting slip, looking as though he could actually write . I had horses picked in the first two races, so I decided to do a double on them and rather than stay in the bookies, I went back home with himself and watched on telly. Jay had this rather large rocking horse at home, complete with saddle and bridle, which were hard to get, by the way, and the only way I could watch the racing in comfort was to set him up on this rocking horse in front of the telly, where he would ride out the finish of each race, he even had the proper whip, so I had to sit well back nearing the finishes.

The two I backed today were both ridden by Pat Eddery (surprise surprise) and the first one was four-to-one joint favourite. I had a ten pound double and after a lot of roaring and shouting, between father and son I had fifty pounds going on to the second race after Eddery had won snugly enough. Jay got down off the rocking horse in the winners' enclosure, just as Pat Eddery did on the telly and I even had to take off the saddle, as everything had to be done correctly. I felt like a right eejit, I can tell you, having to re-saddle the horse for the following race. The things we do!

Race number two and with horses saddled and on the way post, I was praying that Eddery might do me a huge favour on a six-to-one outsider, as the favourite is odds-on. I'd always point out which horse was our one to Jay prior to the race, by showing him the colours and the number. And there's you thinking I was teaching him bad ideas when all the time this was an educational exercise! Pat wore red and white and was on number eight in this race. A five-furlong sprint, which would be over in a matter of minutes and with fifty pounds at six-to-one, the three hundred and fifty back if he won, was like a million to me right now and would be what's known in the game as a nice little touch. I didn't want to tempt faith, however, so I didn't start counting my chickens yet. The race is off and with a furlong to go, the favourite looks like banker material, but Pat Eddery, being one of the very, very best judges of pace, saved every bit of strength from his horse to fight out the last twenty yards and as they passed the post, it was impossible to call the winner, it was so close. "Photo finish, photo finish", Peter O'Sullivan called on the telly. Jesus, it was so tight, that I genuinely didn't know whether I was first or second. It took an eternity to decide the winner and I was sweating, I can tell you. Three hundred and fifty smackers was a nice few bob sixteen years ago, it's even a nice few bob today. Even in my tense state though, I had to laugh as the other lad was on his way to the winners' enclosure with the rocking horse.

'Jesus, I hope you're right, son' I said to him.

Eventually, the result was called: "First number eight". Jesus, I nearly jumped out the window and frightened the life out of the poor child. I was never as happy to unsaddle a rocking horse for the second time in an hour. I gave Jay a high five and he was as happy as I was, which was gas.

The funny thing about it all was that my plan for the day was to have a few bob on what I thought was the bet of the day in the Oaks.

User Friendly, a filly I was very fond of and who'd won for me before. The tenner double was me hoping for a stroke of luck prior to the Oaks, but all of a sudden, my train had come in and now the goalposts had moved and I had a decision to make. Do I collect my few bob and walk away, or do I still back User Friendly? The big race was wide open and even though User Friendly was well-fancied, she was still about eight-to-one in the betting. Either ways, I'd decided that regardless of what I do now, I can't lose once I don't back with the whole lot. There was no fear of this, as this is what the bookies love to see the punter do, as eventually they get it all back if we do. Nothing personal, but I hate bookies! So with mind made up, I strapped Jay in the back seat and drove down and collected my Three-Fifty, decided I'd give Vera a nice few bob as a surprise and had fifty pounds to win on User Friendly at eight-to-one. I had another plan in my head if she won. I had to come back home to watch the race, as the rocking-horse had to be got ready again. Jesus, there were times I could've killed him. I was delighted with the few bob, thanks to Mr. Eddery and as I said regardless, I was in great form. The Oaks was run over a much longer distance than the previous races and in this mile-and-a-half event would you believe, Eddery was one of the favourites, so I thought my goose was cooked from the start. George Duffield had User Friendly right out the back and no way was she winning from there and she was still a long way behind, two furlongs out. I had the little fella shouting "Come on User Friendly" although he couldn't pronounce it properly, but he made a good stab at it. Would you believe it, with a furlong to go, she was flying and passing lots of tired horses, but I still thought, no way can she do it, but the man above was definitely on my side today and yes, she got up to win and for as long as I live, it will long go down as one of my favourite races of all time. 'You little daisy!' I shouted out and Jay said the same to the rocking horse, as we unsaddled for the bloody third time today, thank God. Another four-fifty to collect and no more bets for the day, as nothing was spoiling this special day on me now. My plan, had she won, by the way, was to buy the boot sneakers and have the other lad wearing them for when Mammy came home. They had been described fairly well to me and just in case, I asked the man in the shop if I could change them if they were the wrong ones. Mind you, Jay had to wear them straight away, so I had visions of washing the soles if they were wrong. He was made up with them and I must say they were deadly on him with his jeans.

'Now' says I, 'These are your User Friendly boots, right' and as I said it, the little divil knew well what I meant.

'When is Mammy and Erica coming home?' he asked.

'Why?' says I.

'I want to show them my User Friendly boots' he replied.

Well, he sat on the window ledge with his two feet dangling, with one eye out the window for his Mam and the other one on the boots. I was never as happy to have backed a few horses in all my life as I had today, just looking at him. When Vera got home later, he ran out shouting "look at me User Friendly boots me Daddy bought me".

Vera asked: 'Where did you get the money for them and why in the name of God is he calling them User Friendly?' After I'd explained and given her a few hundred pounds for herself also, she made a huge fuss about them, for which Jay was delighted and while she said the few bob was perfectly-timed, she still said:

'I hope you didn't have that child in the bookies'.

'No' says I, 'I left him at home on his own when I went down'.

She could only laugh. Later that evening, I called out home and the first thing Jay asked my Mam and Dad was: 'Do you like me User Friendly boots?'

My Dad, God bless him, knew straight away that I must have backed her as he'd been watching the race earlier and when he explained the story to Mam, the two of them nearly got sick laughing at the good of it. What a lovely day, what a lovely memory and what a lovely pair of boots. Those boots were worn every day for months and to this day are always fondly called User Friendly boots and will always be one of my wonderful memories of Jay as a child and of having a few bob on the horses. Magic Times!

Fast-forward sixteen years and I am needing another User Friendly to use my luck money on. What's the chances of that happening I ask you?! Maybe the little fella I bought the boots for all those years ago will give me a hand to pick a winner. He's nineteen now instead of three. You know what they say "They don't be long growing up". How true it is.

So I'm studying the form of race after race and having a few trial runs etc. just to see would I have been right or wrong to bet on each one. I was driving myself mad by times if I picked a good winner, but hadn't the money down, mind you, I had picked a lot more losers, so I was nervous as a result and decided to wait and wait. As I said, this money, although it wasn't thousands by any means, but meant an awful lot to me. For weeks, maybe even months, I pondered with *will I or won't I* and in the end decided maybe I'll wait for a big meeting like Cheltenham and have a horse whom I'd follow between now and then and have the money on him or her when the big day came around. It was only a couple of months away as was the beginning of the flat season, which I knew a lot more about, so between the two, I would have my bet then. I backed a few horses in the interim, but my winners and losers were nothing to write home about, so all in all, life was a bit boring to be honest and coupled with nothing but bad news on the economy front and miserable cold weather for January, my motivation levels were only working for day to day, with no great plans or ideas forthcoming. This was also the first year in a long time that I didn't have a filly being prepared for the flat season ahead and this along with being out of work, played havoc on my mind to a certain degree. However, I'd promised myself to embrace 2009 so onwards and upwards regardless.

Your Health
is your Wealth

One thing you can be sure of each year in January is all of the people having the best of intentions for the year ahead. Resolutions of all sorts, but mainly related to health matters, such as increased exercise, or in most cases just some exercise, diets of all descriptions, especially the women. Giving up cigarettes is always in the top five also and for me this has always been the bane of my life. *If I could give up cigarettes, I could do anything.* I've said this for nearly thirty years at this stage. Smoking has always been a disgusting habit and probably one of the most unhealthiest habits one can have. Go to the doctor with whatever complaint you like and nine times out of ten the first thing they will ask you is "Do you smoke?" In my case, the answer to this question has always been "Yes". Times have changed dramatically, however, and smoking has become an almost unacceptable social activity, which I must admit is a good thing. The smoking ban in lots of European countries has been a tremendous success and a welcome relief for those people who worked in public places, such as bars and restaurants and who, as non-smokers, had endured passive smoking all these years. Ireland was the first country to introduce the law and I must say it was a big help to me in cutting back on the number of cigarettes I smoked, as I'm sure it was to many other smokers. In fact, many smokers actually managed to quit completely since the ban was introduced. Much to my surprise, two of my brothers had managed to quit and it gave me some incentive to do likewise. I loved my cigarette, however, and each time I tried, there was always some excuse to go back. I used the hard-luck stories with the horses many a time over the years. There were times such as the fateful night in Dundalk, where I nearly smoked two at a time. All the time I knew though, that in years to come and maybe even the damage to-date would only cause health problems down the line. I remember my first cousin and great friend, who had suffered a severe heart attack at a football match and who very nearly died, prior to having a triple bypass, telling me one evening at another match as I smoked beside him of how foolish I was to be still smoking. He said: 'Skin, don't do like I did and wait for a flashing light of an ambulance as you cling on for dear life to be the reason you give them up'. A sentence that would stay in my mind for months, maybe even over a year and one that still lives with me today. So, and I haven't mentioned this until now purposely, I am now entering my third month off the cigarettes. You weren't expecting that, were you?! YES and I admit I have fallen off the wagon twice and lit one up while having a pint, but each time I decided the following day/week not to smoke. I'm not saying for one minute that I'm sure I've cracked it, but I'm certainly giving it my best shot and as I said, if I can do this, I can do anything.

With the ten days sun on my back from Dubai and with being off the smokes, I have indeed embraced '09 and while there is nothing really exciting from a social perspective going on in my life right now, I have started a type of fitness regime, where I try to eat properly and go for a nice fast walk at least five times a week and spend a few minutes exercising each day. This activity, along with not smoking, is probably the best thing I could have done, or should I say is definitely the best thing I could have done in the current circumstances, although staying away from the cigarettes has made some days, a lot of the days, extremely difficult. My two brothers, who I mentioned earlier, are Eddie, my eldest brother, and Aidan, who is four years younger than me and I'm glad to say that both of them are still non-smokers and have been for a couple of years now. I have always wanted to be able to have a cigarette whenever I have a few drinks etc. but I'm not sure that this will ever be possible, with the result that I've had very few, if any, drinks over the past few months. So one day at a time and let's see what happens. I am now happy to report that I am healthy as I can be with no stress from either work or keeping horses or from smoking, probably because I now have no job, no horse and no cigarettes. It's hard to have it all!

A healthy mind is an active mind, however, and instead of feeling sorry for myself and being miserable, I've used the time to enjoy all the things I like best. Top of the list being enjoying being at home with the family during daylight, followed closely by travelling, such as the trip to Dubai and of course all of the studying and reading up on all things horseracing-related and for the first time ever, I got the chance to go racing mid-week on a few occasions, which I've enjoyed immensely, each time bringing just a small amount of money to cover the day and a few small bets, so that I wouldn't ruin the day by losing that which I currently cannot afford. All the time, mind you, I've been waiting for a sign or an interesting tip etc. to have the luck money on.

I forgot to mention that while in Dubai I had the opportunity to go racing there at their *Nad Al Sheba* racetrack. Nad Al Sheba is home to the Dubai carnival of racing, which begins late January and climaxes with the running of the Dubai World Cup run in March. The meeting I attended at Christmas was just an ordinary meeting, however, but it was a tremendous experience as part of our holiday. First of all, the weather was fabulous with temperatures of 25 degrees Celsius, which was very pleasant to say the least. Secondly, there was no entry fee to the grandstand for the public and entry to the reserved enclosure with bars and restaurants was only seven or eight euro when converted from dyrams. Food and drink prices were much the same as in downtown shops and tables and chairs were made available for everybody. Of course, the biggest difference of the lot was the fact that there was no betting or bookies at the races, which to us westerners, was incredible to see, although we knew beforehand. Mind you, for us Irish, it was also unusual to see free entry at any gate, lots of seating, affordable entry to the enclosure and affordable food inside. I know the Irish authorities can't do much about the weather, but my personal opinion is that there may well be lots of good ideas to be learned in how the authorities in Dubai go out of their way to ensure patrons have a very pleasant and comfortable day's racing. There was a very large crowd there as a result, on, as I said, what was just an ordinary day's racing. It was also an interesting experience for us dressed as we do among the Arabian dressed public in their full attire. Let's just say it was easy enough to find each other and would you believe, just because there was no betting, Jay and I picked five of the six race winners. Typical. A lot of European jockeys from the flat spend their winters there and one of the winners was ridden by Shane Gorey, would you believe, who used to ride A Chuisle on the flat for us. Dubai is a far cry from a wet and windy Navan, I can tell you.

Sixth Sense

"What's for you won't pass you by"

For some unknown reason, this saying has been doing a bloody jig in my head from the very second I heard it from Paddy in Cork, after I left the horse down to him. For some unknown reason also, I felt something strange, I use the word strange in the nicest possible sense (and for the want of a better word) about the man. A sort of sixth sense that I detected from him as soon as I met the man. It was as though he was hiding something or keeping some unknown secret to himself, even though he could not have been nicer and more friendly to me than he was. It's difficult to explain how exactly I felt and it's never happened me before, but as I drove away that day I was saying to myself - *Some strange little thing about this transaction?* Don't get me wrong. I didn't think it was anything dark or sinister or even anything great. It was just some strange little thing.

This few bob luck money in the meantime still remained in the jug and for me to hold onto money for even more than one day was strange. It was beginning to feel more and more like Jack's beans as the days went by. I was half-afraid that some morning I'd wake up to find a huge tree growing out from the jug up through the presses and out through the roof. Now I'm really losing it, I thought! Anyway, there was no tree after all, but the whole thing felt a little peculiar to me.

In the meantime, I was anxious to know how the horse was getting on in her new home and was hoping above all that she was behaving herself. I still had Paddy's phone number, so one night I decided to give him a ring out of both interest and courtesy, to ask how the horse was. A lady answered the phone and I took it to be Paddy's wife and I asked if Paddy was in and could I speak to him, having said hello. The lady seemed a little nervous, or even taken aback and asked who was calling. I explained who I was and about the horse etc. and she said she was delighted to hear from me. She then explained that Paddy was a bit under the weather and probably not up to taking the call, so I apologised and explained that I just wanted to check how the horse was getting on with them and indeed them with her. Out of the blue, she said:

'God, it's an awful pity, he would have loved to have a chat with you'.

She then continued in the same breath and proceeded to tell me how "the horse was the best thing that ever came into the place". She even put the phone on loudspeaker and called her teenage daughter and both of them took turns at telling me how much they loved the horse and how she was so easy to manage and such a great jumper and such a pet and how daddy (meaning Paddy) was stone-mad about her and called her 'his little chicken', which stuck me to the floor for a second as that's what I had always called her as a pet, as you know. The young girl then said that she loved A Chuisle to bits and because of the name A Chuisle, she herself caller her her Million Dollar Baby, as in the film, which she explained in full to me, not knowing of course, that this is how she got her name in the first place, but I didn't dare spoil either her or her Dad's pet names for the horse. As a matter of fact, I was thrilled that they were so fond of her and so thankful even a few months later to me for letting them have her. I told them I'd ring again sometime and hoped Paddy might be feeling better when I did. The woman thanked me for the call and went out of her way to explain how they really appreciated me going to the bother of enquiring on the horse.

'I'm so sorry Paddy can't talk to you because he's done nothing but sing your praises since you drove out of the yard that day'.

'Ah, tell him thanks very much and give him my regards' I said.

On putting down the phone, I remember feeling really, really good and little bit emotional for some reason. I think it was a mixture of the love they obviously had for the horse and the fact that the poor man was obviously ill. Anyway, I was feeling relieved that all was well with the horse. I was even more confused about the strange feelings I had having met the man, as I didn't get to speak to him tonight and I wondered was he just sick with a bug for a few days, or was it more serious, but I certainly wasn't going to ask. Either ways, I told the woman I would keep in touch and ring her again, at which stage I could hopefully have a chat with Paddy. In the course of the telephone conversation, the young girl had mentioned that her Dad was as fond of the horse as he was about his teaching job, from which he had retired early. She said that nothing had cheered him up as much since he'd retired. Knowing how happy the horse had made him feel had me looking forward to ringing him at a later date. I remember thinking that my sixth sense was probably just detecting the fact that I'd met such a lovely man and his family, whom I always knew would really take good care of the horse.

My Saturday

The following morning being Saturday, I remember waking up full of the joys of spring in the middle of winter. No job, no cigs, no horse, don't ask me why I awoke in such good form. I sang at breakfast, I sang as I shaved and I was like Pavarotti in the shower. I remember putting my arm around Erica and saying:

'Ah, it's great to be alive, Nick'.

I had no plans for the day, which is the way I like Saturdays to be. The weather was crisp and dry and bitterly cold, following a night's frost. I decided to have a walk as I do now most mornings and the fact is that I don't have much choice, as since I've been out of work, my West Highland terrier Peggy Sue (yes, that's her real name) is waiting for me and watching my every move as soon as I open the kitchen door. She sits and stares up at me while I have breakfast and as soon as she knows I'm ready, she runs around in circles like a mad woman, until I get out her lead and head off. I normally walk for an hour or so and on Saturday mornings I pick up my copy of The Irish Field in The Corner Newsstand. This Saturday was no different and on my return I sat down with a cuppa and had a quick look at the day's racing cards and had a glance through the headlines of The Field, which I would read in full, later in the day. Racing in Ireland today was in Naas and there were lots of meetings on from the UK. No race or horse in particular jumped off the page at me, but before I relaxed for the afternoon, I drove down to the bookies as I had it in my mind to do, maybe a yankee or multiple bet of some description, to cover a few races which I would watch at home in the afternoon. I had all my jobs done around the house from earlier in the week, so I looked forward to a relaxing afternoon in front of the telly, watching the races and in between races I'd catch up on the weekly news from The Irish Field.

A few of the lads were in the bookies and I had a chat with them in general and proceeded to discuss our selections for the day. The usual banter and of course the usual few tips from the various sources were all put forward. I was still in great form and had my mind made up not to speculate too much and just do the few small bets just for interest sake more than anything. All of the afternoon's racing was National Hunt and the only flat racing was actually live on SIS from South Africa's Turfonteine track. It's hard enough trying to pick a winner from Ireland or the UK, where I'd have some clue of form without trying to pick a winner from South Africa, but just as I was about to leave, having speculated my twenty euro on a yankee and a double, I overheard a name from the live South African coverage for their upcoming race, which was due off in ten minutes or so and the horses were about to leave the parade ring on their way to post. The horses name which had caught my attention was *Teacher's Life* and the reason it struck me was because I thought of the luck money from Paddy the ex-teacher from Cork and I'd waited for a good tip or a sign of some description for months at this stage and the money was gathering dust in the bowl at home by now. Was this the sign I was waiting for? Was I losing the bit of sense I had? I don't know, but it was possible to bet on the race from South Africa and I remember thinking that if that horse wins and I don't back him, I will eat my you-know-what! I waited for the betting to come through and when it did it was a wide-open betting event. A seven-furlong handicap on the turf, with the favourite priced at six-to-one and Teacher's Life put in at odds of ten to one. I did notice that Teacher's Life was running in his first handicap, having run well in his previous maiden race on the same track. The only reason I noticed this was because the commentator mentioned it! In an instant I decided *fuck, here goes.* I checked with the girls at the counter if I could have three hundred euros on a horse in Turfontaine at odds of ten to one and not having the money with me, could they take the bet on credit till I got back down in case I was too late, as the race would soon be off. Being a regular, the girls had no problem with this, so I wasn't changing my mind now and filled out my docket. *€300 win Teacher's Life 10/1*, with time of the race and the name of the meeting, which I abbreviated to Turf. The girl kept the docket and I rushed out the door and said I'd be back in five minutes. I flew home, grabbed the €300 from the jug, leaving one hundred there just in case and was back in the bookies all paid up, just as the last horse was loaded and would you believe who it was only Teacher's Life! *And they're off!* I hasten to add that I never put that much on normally, unless I'm winning a fortune and even then I'd be reluctant, but this was different, it was as though someone was telling me what to do, or as I say maybe I was just losing the run of myself for a few minutes. Either way, the money was down, so there was no turning back now. For some reason, I wasn't even nervous watching the race, nor did I even tell anyone else that I'd put so much on a fuckin' handicap race in South Africa of all places. I didn't even know one horse in the race and even worse again I never heard of any of the jockeys before. I remember thinking for a second that there's places for people like me, but there's three furlongs gone at this point, so I better start watching to see where the hell is this horse of mine in a field of twelve. He's going grand actually, just sitting back in fourth position and travelling nicely. Rounding the bend at the five marker and he's still in fourth. As the pace increases, he's right there with them and for a second I think 'Oh, why the fuck didn't I back him each-way?' as he was guaranteed to be in the first three from here on in, which would have guaranteed me a quarter of the odds on a stake of €150. I'm talking to myself at the furlong pole.

'Come on jockey, whoever the fuck you are, give him a slap' and fair play to him, he did, to which the Teacher responded immediately and quickly moved two lengths ahead and was pulling up in front passing the winning post.

Three thousand, three hundred fuckin' euro back!

'Holy Divine, I'm never studying form again' was my first instinctive reaction. I just couldn't believe it. I knew there was something about Paddy from Cork. He gave me what he said was luck money and I can't get much luckier than this right now, I'm thinking. I think I'm in shock! It's funny actually, when I came out and got into the car, there was a Bruce Springsteen song playing on the radio when I turned the ignition. The funny thing was that I'd never heard the song before and for me this is unusual, because I know every song the man ever sang. I listened carefully to try to identify the song, only to find out it's a brand-new single, to be released from his new album and the name of the song is *Working on a Dream*. I've just come from the bookies working on my own dream and thinking, with the way trade in bloodstock is at present, that my few grand win might just go a long way towards buying a winning mare-in-foal in the breeding sales in February at Goffs and allowing me to start right back at the beginning, but this time knowing ten times more than I knew before. The words of the song are going something like: 'I'm working on a dream, but sometimes it seems so far away, working on a dream and I know I'll make it real someday!' or something to that effect, but you know what I mean, this is all a bit surreal, between the luck money possibly making my dream a distinct possibility again, when I thought all was lost and then my idol Bruce Springsteen writing a song to be played for the first time on radio today, five minutes after my win and sounding as though the song was written for me almost. I don't know, maybe I'm just in a dream right now, or maybe I'm just losing the plot, full-stop.

When I arrived home, the house was empty as they were all gone away somewhere. I put on the kettle and made myself a cup of tea, sat down and enjoyed the moment. Three grand was a nice, tidy sum, but it wasn't really the amount, but more the manner in which it came about. I definitely felt as though the whole thing was some sort of sign, telling me not to give up now and I am in no way superstitious and as I sat back enjoying my tea, the words *What's for you won't pass you* by did a jig around my brain. I needed a cigarette, but remembered I'm off them, so I made do with a biscuit instead. When the others came home, they thought I was joking, as they knew all about the luck money etc. but they would not believe me until I counted the money out on the table.

'What are you gonna do with the money?' they asked.

'I might just buy myself a mare in foal next month' I replied, and three voices at the one time were heard saying:

'Oh Lord Jesus, here we go again!'

It was so funny for the three of them to say the very same thing in unison and all we could do was laugh.

'I'm not saying I will for definite, until I see the catalogue' I said.

I gave each of them a few bob and told them to have a drink on me and the bulk of the few bob would go to the bank on the following Monday. I could see by them that they were delighted for me. I picked up my Irish Field from the magazine rack and lying beside it was the catalogue from Goffs – November foal sale on the back of which, written in gold writing, was *Your Dream is Our Dream*. When I saw it, I grinned and thought to myself 'It sure is'. Would you believe it, later that evening I collected two hundred and twenty back on my twenty euro bet. What's seldom is wonderful and I hope for one minute that I'm not encouraging anybody to gamble to make their fortune, as it is far easier to pick losers rather than winners. Remember Joe's rusty bike!

That night I decided to treat herself to a nice meal and a few drinks following my good fortune. As I drove to the restaurant, I said:

'All I need now is for the job I want to come along and I'll be on the pig's back'.

'Here's hoping' she replied.

One way or the other, regardless, nothing was going to ruin my day, which from the very second I got out of bed that morning had been wonderful. I was starving by the time we had dinner and as we waited for coffee, my phone rang with private number displayed on my caller

ID. I answered and wasn't sure of the lady's voice at the other end. She asked 'Is that Brendan?' and when I said it was, she told me it was 'Mrs. Kelly, from Cork, Paddy's wife', 'Paddy, who you brought the horse down to' she explained. I never even knew Paddy had the same surname as me, so it took me a second to realise who she was, until she mentioned the horse.

'I hope you don't mind me ringing and disturbing you at this hour' she said.

'Not at all' says I.

'I'm afraid we said goodbye to Paddy earlier today' she said, 'and I thought it only right to let you know after all you did and after your lovely phone call last night'.

I wanted the ground to swallow me up right there and then as I did not know what to say to her.

'Oh my God, Mrs. Kelly, I'm so sorry, when you said last night that he was ill, I thought it might be just flu or the likes, I didn't realise'.

'There's no need to apologise' she said. 'If it wasn't for your bringing the horse down he'd have been gone a couple of months by now and would never have got to see the young one here become so good at her and his beloved show-jumping. He had been given only weeks to live when you met him the first day and that little filly of yours kept him going for the last couple of months. He didn't tell you because he didn't like to talk about it'.

Once again, I said I was so sorry to hear and offered my condolences. She said 'I'll leave you be for now, as you're probably out for a drink, but I had to let you know and above all, I just wanted to say thanks on behalf of us all and please don't worry about the filly, she'll be very well-looked after'.

All I could say was 'No problem at all and I hope you're ok' at which point she said goodbye and God bless. When I hung up the call, I had a tear in my eye and a lump in my throat, as I thought to myself that I knew there was something about that lovely man that I couldn't put my finger on and then I thought, how ironic it was, of all the days for me to choose to use the luck money from Paddy, God bless him. When I told Vera, she was amazed also. I finished my coffee and went home and I couldn't sleep that night, following the sad end to a wonderful day.

The following morning I checked the death notices in the newspaper to see that Paddy's funeral would be on Monday morning, so I decided to head to Cork that evening and stay overnight and attend the following day. I felt I really had to and really wanted to show my respects. I stayed in a B&B close to the church and Monday morning at eleven o' clock mass I was there. There was a huge turnout for the funeral and it was quite obvious to me that I wasn't the only person to think that Paddy was a lovely man. I called over to shake hands with Mrs. Kelly following the burial and as soon as I did, she knew me.

'Oh, my God, you didn't come all that way to be here today? That's not why I rang you, I just wanted to let you know. Oh, I can't believe you came all this way'.

'You're fine' I replied. 'I just felt I should'.

She would not release my hand and she called: 'Caroline, Caroline, will you look who called down, it's the young man who owned the horse'. The young girl to her left was her daughter and the young girl who Paddy wanted the horse for.

'Oh, I'm so pleased to meet you, Daddy never stopped talking about how good you were to let us have her and she made him so happy for the last couple of months. We can't thank you enough and I swear we love her to bits and we'll mind her like a child'.

She was a lovely young girl so I told her I couldn't be happier with who has the horse and I told her to take care of herself and how sorry I was for her loss. The two of them hugged me and invited me to join them at the local hotel following the funeral, but I declined as I felt they had more than enough people to talk to. I told them I needed to get back, which I did and it was long road ahead.

'Goodbye and God bless and please keep in touch' they said.

I said I would and walked away. I had been made most welcome at such a sad time for them and they had made me feel so good about myself in their appreciation of the horse, that it almost made me glad of the way things had turned out.

Conclusion

So, after all of this, I still don't have my own winner, but I've made somebody happy at least and above all, I have all of the stories to tell, which at the end of the day are worth more to me than anything. I'm not giving up by any means and I'll be in Goffs next month to begin my quest from scratch all over again. Hopefully there'll be lots more stories to tell and I'll leave you with my favourite one of all. I've been keeping the best till last.

A few years ago, we, as in my Da and I, were on our annual pilgrimage to Cheltenham. To us, this didn't mean going to the actual races, but our annual trip to Cheltenham meant four afternoons in Anderson's Pub, watching the racing from Cheltenham, having a few pints, a few bets and bit of fun, a lot of fun. This particular year, there were lots of us in the pub and the place was buzzin'. Three or four of my brothers, Siobhan, Mary, Vera, Jason, Erica, plus a few of my nieces and nephews, they were all there. Lots of Dad's friends were there also, including Keith Granger, a son of my first cousin Rose and a great young friend to my Da. My brother-in-law Johnny Pender was there also, so basically the scene was set for a major session. As it turned out, we backed a right few winners, even Aidan (Nay) backed a winner and that's a first, so the craic was ninety and the pints of Guinness were flowing fast and furious. This I remind you was a once-a-year event. I wouldn't want anybody thinking we were out drinking and backing horses every day! However, as the day progressed, we were all well-jarred and in flying form and we'd won a nice few quid. With just one race left, Da told the whole pub that he had a certainty for the last race. We asked him what it was and he gave us some name and it was agreed among a lot of drunken people that everybody in the pub would back this horse, just for the laugh. It was only when Dad saw the amount of twenty-notes and even the odd fifty-note been handed about for bets that he was sorry he opened his mouth at all. We all told him it was his fault if the horse doesn't win. All the bets were written out on the blank dockets we had from the bookies and the bar owner John kept account of names and how much per person, mainly because John was the only sober person in the pub. Well, Da was a bag of nerves when the race started and you could cut the tension with a knife as we all watched. There was such excitement that the horses were not the only thing racing, every heart in the pub was racing also. You can imagine the excitement as they approached the last hurdle and the horse we were all on was about four lengths clear. He skipped over it as though it wasn't there and immediately the cheers went up and we were shouting 'Go on, Har Kelly!' as the horse sprinted past the winning post. My Da had made the remark of having a certainty more off the cuff than anything and was a relieved man by now, but he was shaking with excitement. The lads shook hands with him and clapped his back etc. because the horse was twelve-to-one and some of us had a lot to collect, so much so that the bookies were nearly cleaned out. Just as people settled down and got their breaths back, my Da, who was centre circle at this point said first of all: 'Didn't I tell yee?' but the funny thing was, this was nearly half an hour after the race and it had taken this long before he could even talk, which made everybody laugh, but then he brought the house down altogether when he asked John:

'Hey John, do you sell shorts?'

John answered: 'Course we sell shorts, Har'.

'Well, will you give me out a pair, because I think I need to change my trousers'.

Well, between what he'd said and how he'd said it, the place erupted and some people laughed at it so much, that they had to go outside for air, including myself.

Well, looking back on this day just confirms that while financially I got nothing back yet from the horses, nor have I had that elusive winner, but my time with horses has given me far more than any money could ever buy. My Dad may no longer be with us, but I know he's looking down and I can never thank him enough for making me fall in love with the 'sport of kings'. There are far too many other people to thank, but I can't finish without thanking all of the friends who have become involved in the various syndicates with me over the years and who knows, when things pick up, we might go again. I pay special thanks to the trainers, who worked with the horses and gave me the opportunity of working on my dream and seeing our colours on the track. I'll continue to dream of leading in my own winner and hearing *'Winner Alright, Winner Alright'* announced over the intercom, but thanks to the great times I've had, both in growing up and in racing to-date, I can say with my hand on my heart that *'Skinner's Alright'*.

Thank you for sharing my story. I hope you've enjoyed reading it as much as I've enjoyed living it.